LOBSTER ON A CHEESE PLATE

LOBSTER ON A CHEESE PLATE

HOW TO STAND OUT, ATTRACT THE BEST CLIENTS, AND WIN EVERY SALE THAT COMES YOUR WAY

MARK HARARI

Lobster on a Cheese Plate: How to stand out, attract the best clients, and win every sale that comes your way

Published by
Remodelers Advantage Inc.
514 Progress Drive, Suite S
Linthicum, MD 21090
www.remodelersadvantage.com

ISBN: 978-0-578-74635-7
Library of Congress Control Number: 2020915452

Cover design by Alexander Vulchev
Book design by Sue Balcer

Printed in the United States of America
10 9 8 7 6 5 4 3 2 1

Visit www.BeTheLobster.com

To my Jake and Sophie.
You can be anything you want in this world,
but whatever you choose,
be the lobster.

Table of Contents

Foreword

If your goal is to build a valuable company then you are in the right place. Having a crisp point of differentiation helps you in two ways. First, a well-differentiated company with unique products has pricing authority, which allows you to make better profit margins. If you pour some of that extra cash into further differentiating your business, you'll create a competitive moat, making it difficult for rivals to compete with you.

Being different is also one of the most important drivers of your company's value. Whether you want to sell soon or in a decade or two, an acquirer will only be interested in buying your business if it's well differentiated from your competitors.

Differentiation usually comes down to better marketing. It's equal parts art and science, and many small business owners get lost in trying to balance the two. They're focused on sales, but they've forgotten about branding. They have a great product or service, but their messaging doesn't resonate with their ideal customer. Or they're trying too hard to be all things to everyone, and lose their identity along the way.

These days, my work involves helping small business owners build value into their companies, and often the necessary steps include taking a hard look at their marketing. For many of those owners, the process of building a marketing plan is a mystery. They leap straight over questions of brand identity, niche markets, and points of differentiation and go straight to cookie-cutter marketing "solutions" like "We should build a new website" and "We need to be on social media."

The problem is, without answering the fundamental question of how your business is different from all your competitors—whether they're other small businesses like yours, franchises with a recognizable brand name behind them, or international powerhouses—all you'll wind up with is a website that could be promoting anyone's product or service and social media accounts with no clear message that quickly fall by the wayside, further hurting your credibility.

If your attempts to define your brand and to build a marketing plan that works have resulted in endless false starts or dead-end tactics like a mailing list you haven't reached out to in months, then I'm so glad you're holding this book.

Lobster on a Cheese Plate is equal parts how-to manual and textbook. Yes, Mark has put together a number of useful templates and guides that will help you build the identity and messaging you'll need to successfully market your business, but more fundamentally, he's laid out a roadmap by which you can build a complete brand identity.

Not to say that getting to the end of the map won't involve some work, but *Lobster on a Cheese Plate* gives you a springboard with real-world examples to show effective methods in action, along with some great pop-culture references to keep you entertained.

If you follow the roadmap all the way to the end, you'll discover that the journey has given you not only a robust marketing plan but also a clearer idea of who you are in the marketplace—as well as where to find those lobster-loving customers you've been waiting for. And that kind of positioning is truly priceless.

John Warrillow
Founder, The Value Builder System
Author of *Built to Sell* and *The Automatic Customer*

Preface

I must confess, this book was originally titled *Marvelous Marketing: A step-by-step guide to differentiate and dominate in any economy.* (I make a number of references to the Marvel movies, so Marvelous Marketing seemed like a good way to go).

But every time I read it I heard Billy Crystal saying *Mahvelous Mahketing, dahling.*

My second choice, *How to Win Every Client in Any Economy Regardless of Price*, was pretty strong, but it didn't make the final cut either. Even though that's precisely what you'll learn, many thought it sounded like a book for salespeople.

Understandable.

A book that promises to help you win every client *must* be a sales training manual. But this is not. It's a book on marketing. More specifically, it's a book on *marketing that helps small, service-based businesses stand out and dominate their market, regardless of whether they compete in a market saturated with similar service companies, or franchises and corporations thousands of times their size.*

Of course, that wouldn't fit on the cover.

In the end I decided on a MacGuffin. If you're not familiar with the term, a MacGuffin is a plot device that propels the action while being irrelevant in itself. In essence it's the motivation, the thing the hero is chasing after, but which has nothing to do with his journey.

It's the suitcase in *Pulp Fiction*, the Dude's rug in *The Big Lebowski*, and "Rosebud" in *Citizen Kane.* They're all MacGuffins.

The lobster on a cheese plate is my hero's MacGuffin. (That's you.) It's a vivid illustration of how you will differentiate yourself from competitors after putting what you learn from this book into practice. But, like any good MacGuffin, it's served its purpose once the journey is underway.

So don't expect to see many mentions of lobsters and cheese after the introduction. (Though I do talk about cheese*burgers* at one point.)

One impression you may have gotten, particularly with the second title option, is the implication that good marketing can replace a salesperson. I am not suggesting that. What I *am* saying is that marketing—when done as I lay out in this book—can connect with your client so strongly that signing them is virtually guaranteed before the salesperson even says hello.

Yes, marketing can be *that* powerful. I've witnessed it, firsthand, time and time again. I've been using variations of the techniques in this book since my early days in marketing (and I'm no spring chicken).

I started my marketing career in 1999 with a freelance side hustle and never looked back. I've since spent the better part of the past quarter-century running marketing programs for a number of small businesses. I'm also a marketing consultant, speaker, and facilitator of a mastermind program for marketers.

Although it's true that the majority of these endeavors has been in the construction industry, I can tell you that, in no uncertain terms, this process works for everyone from attorneys to pet sitters and every business in between.

While I wish I could say I invented everything in this book, I did not. Though there are some concepts and techniques that are my own, the truth is that much of what you'll learn here are proven methods that have been used for decades by some of the largest, most successful companies on the planet.

But that's really the point.

These companies have teams of marketing PhDs and high-dollar agencies to work their magic. You have you. So I've boiled it down into an easy-to-read, easy-to-execute process that a business owner or solo-marketer can do on their own.

It's the same process I've used with great success for many years. I hope you enjoy the same.

Introduction

**I've been fighting with one arm tied behind my back.
What happens when I'm finally set free?**

—Carol Danvers, Captain Marvel

You have an amazing company. Your service is exceptional. Your passion is unmatched, and it shows. Sure, there are others who offer a similar service, but you are by far the best choice. So where are all the leads? And why aren't you converting all of the leads you do get into paying customers?

One word: cheese.

Let me explain. Actually, that would take a whole book. Let me sum up.

Imagine a day in the life of a Harley-Davidson salesperson. He doesn't spend one moment of his precious time selling people on why they should buy a Harley. They have already decided that if they're buying a bike, it's going to be a Harley.

The salesperson's job is not to sell the Harley-Davidson brand. It's to find the right bike for the buyer and upsell and cross-sell as much as possible along the way.

The same thing goes for Apple. You won't walk into an Apple store and see their salespeople going round after round with customers on why an iPhone is better than a Samsung Galaxy. They're explaining the differences in the models and going over color options.

How do Harley-Davidson and Apple pull that off? How are prospects sold before they walk into the store?

Simple. They're not cheese.

Not that there's anything wrong with cheese. I love cheese. From cheddar to gouda to goat to brie, there isn't a cheese I don't like. And put a cheese plate in front of me? Fuggedaboutit.

Of course, therein lies the rub. A cheese plate is a land of slightly different good choices, none of which scream, "Pick me!" And so I must be convinced. Sometimes, the deciding factor is circumstance—cubes of toothpicked cheddar are easier for a drive-by pluck at the kitchen island. Other times, presentation will win, enticing me to select a warm brie trickling from its rind over a wedge of blue cheese. It just depends. My choice off the plate is unpredictable and changes from one day to the next.

But put some lobster on the cheese plate, and the choice is clear. It's exotic and unexpected. Besides, on a plate of assorted cheese, lobster will be the first thing to go. There's only one obvious choice, at least to people who like lobster.

And that's the secret. All you have to do, to stand out and attract the best clients, is be the lobster on a cheese plate.

So how do you become the lobster of your market? Well, at the risk of alienating an entire profession, consider what sales is for a moment. At its core, selling comes down to answering one simple question: *Why should I choose you*?

The best answer wins.

But there's a catch. Your prospect starts answering that question *on your behalf* from the moment he or she becomes aware of your existence (i.e., the moment he or she sees the cheese plate).

If all your prospect sees is a wedge of cheddar among the other varieties of cheese, then you're nothing more than one of many slightly different good choices on the plate. Indeed, you can still win the client, but it's far less predictable.

This book will show you how to be the lobster on that cheese plate, the obvious choice from the onset. Becoming so will dramatically shorten your sales cycle, increase your close rate, and allow your sales team to focus on the only thing that counts, to "get them to sign on the line that is dotted," as Blake in *Glengarry Glen Ross* would say.

What This Book Is and What It Isn't

This book is not a bunch of fluff and conjecture, peddling abstract marketing theory and principles at you. It is a practical guide that uses real-world examples and comes complete with interactive lessons, exercises, and free tools for download. By the end, you'll have a business ready to dominate your market, regardless of whom you compete with.

I've broken down the process of "lobstering your business" into five sections. It is very much linear, with each chapter building on the one before. Section One focuses on information gathering and research. Admittedly, it is the least interactive, but it lays the foundation for everything to come. It's possible that some of the later exercises will ask you a question that you can't answer, and that's where what you learn in this critical first section comes to the rescue.

In Section Two, we roll up our sleeves and get to work on your business. With a little help from the Marvel movies, you'll discover what truly makes you unique, and learn how to differentiate yourself from the competition. We'll identify your perfect client, what that client's *real* needs are, and how you can fill that need in a way no one else can.

Section Three is dedicated to communicating what you've discovered about yourself to the world. You'll learn how to craft a message that resonates with your target and leaves no doubt in their minds that you are the clear and obvious choice.

Of course, as Yogi Berra once said, "If you don't know where you are going, you'll end up someplace else." So, in Section Four, you learn the six-step process to creating a strategic marketing plan that will not only get you where you're going, but do so with the highest return on your marketing dollar.

And finally, Section Five delves into the successful implementation and execution of all that you have built. We'll look at a handful of specific tactics in great detail—tactics that virtually every business will use, regardless of strategy—and we'll look at how to do it all alone since, odds are, you're operating as a marketing department of one.

If my calculations are correct, when you finish implementing this baby, you're going to see some serious shit.

A Warning

I own a t-shirt that declares me "fluent in sarcasm and movie quotes." It was a birthday present from my business partner. She pretty much nailed it—I'm guilty as charged. While I believe I've successfully held my sarcasm at bay during the writing of this manuscript, something had to give. So, I tend to drop in movie quotes and indirect references from time to time. (Like the one above).

Don't worry. It won't be necessary for you to have seen the films I mention to get the point I'm making. Consider it a bonus that you're getting free movie recommendations from yours truly (because I never quote bad flicks).

Now that that's out of the way, let's make you a lobster.

[SECTION ONE]

GECKOS DON'T EAT CHEESE

The most valuable commodity
I know of is information.

—Gordon Gekko, *Wall Street*

ONE
THE FOUNDATION OF YOUR SUCCESS

KNOWLEDGE IS THE FOUNDATION OF EVERY SUCCESSFUL endeavor, and marketing is no exception. To successfully implement all that you learn in this book, you must understand what your customers think and feel. And I'm not just talking about what they think about the services you offer. I'm talking about everything.

What scares them? What excites them? What do they do for fun? The deeper your understanding, the more successful you will be in becoming the lobster.

That is why customer research needs to be an ongoing part of your marketing program. Unfortunately, many small business owners believe that market research is a costly proposition involving extensive and ongoing resources—something reserved for "big business." But those who think this way have fallen victim to one of the classic blunders. (The most famous blunder, as you may know, is getting involved in a land war in Asia.) But only slightly less well known is this: market research should be conducted by companies of any size, even solopreneurs.

It's only through research that you will be able to make well-informed business decisions. Everything from what color your logo should be to how much you should charge for your services can be gleaned from the results. A deep understanding of your target customer also happens to be vital to effective positioning, which we will be spending a significant amount of time on in Section Two.

A word of caution, however. It's (almost) impossible to conduct market research without asking for a favor, because getting *valuable* feedback is an imposition on someone's time. So the key to an effective research program—especially for a small business—is to be judicious and deliberate with your efforts.

In the following chapters, we'll look at the two types of research methods, quantitative and qualitative, and how to use them effectively to get the valuable information you need to build an unstoppable marketing machine. Don't worry—the fancy names are as technical as it gets.

TWO
NUMBERS DON'T LIE, BUT DO THEY TELL THE TRUTH?

WHEN SOMEONE SAYS MARKET RESEARCH, YOU MOST likely think of surveys. And surveys are a form of quantitative research. Often referred to as *quant*, quantitative research is all about measurement and numbers. The focus is on collecting *statistically significant* data. In other words, we want to get accurate data that will scale.

You see quant in action every time you watch a baseball game. Consider a baseball player whose batting average is .250. This means you can expect him to get a hit 25 percent of the time, or once at every four at bats. Easy, right? But what if this player is a rookie and has only had four at bats in his entire career? That's hardly proof that he's a .250 hitter. The sample size is too small, and as such, the data isn't statistically significant.

The same is true of your quant research; if the sample size is too small, your results will likely reflect randomness instead of conclusiveness, and you can't make well-informed business decisions based on random results.

How large of a sample size do you need for your quant research to be useful? Simple. You need thirty responses. Why? I don't know. I'm not a statistician. All I know is that the French mathematician Pierre-Simon Laplace first proved the *central limit theorem*, which states that if a sample size (referred to as n) is large enough, the distribution will be "approximately normal." And, according to our French friend, the general rule is that *n* be greater than or equal to thirty.

Which brings me to the biggest challenge small businesses face in using quant: it all comes down to your survey response rate. If you can manage to get a whopping 50 percent of the people you ask to take the survey, then you would need a pool of sixty people in order to achieve the requisite thirty responses. However, if your response rate is a lowly 5 percent, then you would need a pool of 600 people to get the thirty responses. Some businesses don't have sixty clients to survey, much less 600.

It becomes even more challenging if you want to segment the results. For example, you may want to compare men to women, or compare age groups, or compare by marital status, and so on. You'll need a minimum of thirty responses per segment to get reliable results that will scale. This means that, for some companies, you won't be able to use quant because you won't have a large enough pool to draw from.

But all is not lost. If you don't think you're able to pull off statistically significant results from your available pool of respondents, you still have qualitative research to lean on.

THREE
IT'S NICE TO BE A FLY ON THE QUAL

TO REALLY UNDERSTAND YOUR CUSTOMERS, YOU NEED to look beyond the numbers. And for that, we turn to qualitative research methods. Often shortened to *qual*, qualitative research focuses on understanding meanings and concepts. So where quant is about numbers, qual is about words.

Because of this, it's important to know that statistical significance is not possible with qual. But that's okay, because this type of research is for understanding the why behind the numbers. Let me explain by way of example.

Let us suppose that through a survey, you discover that 80 percent of your customers are dog owners. That's a fascinating revelation, but it has no meaning. You know *what* they are (dog owners), but you don't know *why*.

Why are dog owners more attracted to your business than non-dog owners? A quantitative survey can't answer that question. It's just a bunch of numbers. So we would use a qualitative method to find out.

Let's dive into some of the types of qualitative methods you can use to learn more about the why behind your customers thinking.

One-on-One Interviews

The first method is one that you've probably already used without even realizing it: the one-on-one interview. This is, as the name implies, a conversation between you and the customer. And it doesn't have to be face-to-face. A phone call is perfectly acceptable. While it may seem counterintuitive to spend so much time with only one person, in the world of qual, an *n of one* can be highly beneficial. To hear the inflections of someone's voice and read their body language as they respond provides layers upon layers of information that a written survey response never could.

Additionally, the benefit to a free-flowing conversation is that you never know where it will lead. This can provide insights you may never have imagined. And because of the significant amount of information that can be ascertained from a single interview, having as few as five responses per segment is usually enough to get a clear picture of what you're looking to learn.

A word of caution: one-on-one interviews are particularly susceptible to the desirability bias. This is a person's impulse to say what they think you want to hear. It's our innate motivation to be liked that's at fault.

This bias is easily overcome in anonymous surveys because they're…well, anonymous. But when speaking one-on-one, this desire manifests itself and skews your results.

For example, a real estate agent approaches a client after she goes to settlement on her new house and asks if there was anything he could have done to improve the client's home-buying experience. In truth, the client feels that the agent took too long to respond to emails, even having complained to her husband about it on more than one occasion. But now that the transaction is over, she doesn't see the benefit in sharing this criticism, especially at the risk of offending the agent and having him dislike her. So she doesn't mention it.

There isn't much you can do to avoid this from happening, save addressing the elephant in the room ahead of time and explicitly giving them permission to be blunt. You could also consider giving a specific example of how a past client's candor helped you improve.

For instance, "Please be honest. You won't hurt my feelings. I'm always striving to improve. Case in point, I used to respond to client emails with text messages thinking it was faster. But a client once told me that it drove him crazy because he couldn't refer back to his email. So, I don't do that anymore."

Focus Groups

Another powerful tool to discover the why behind your customers' thinking is the focus group. In the most basic terms, a focus group is a discussion between a facilitator and a small group of participants. This means that success is dependent on the facilitator's ability to manage and interact with the group.

A good facilitator must do the following:

- Create an environment of trust and openness.
- Create, establish, and enforce ground rules.
- Be respectful and nonjudgmental.
- Be a good listener and communicator.
- Be Switzerland (don't choose sides or endorse opinions).
- Be able to limit participants that dominate the conversation.
- Be able to get the quiet and timid to contribute.
- Defuse disagreements if they occur.

Good planning is key to running a successful focus group. Here are some things to keep in mind as you prepare:

1. Keep it small. Six to ten participants tends to be the sweet spot. This ensures everyone will participate, and it gives you the ability to probe deeper into the discussions. Always

invite a couple more than the minimum to protect against last-minute cancellations.

2. Keep it short. Two hours is just about perfect. With the first half-hour typically spent on housekeeping items, such as welcoming your guests, going over the ground rules, and attendee introductions, it leaves you ninety minutes to get to the heart of the conversation.
3. Keep it relaxed. Your role as the facilitator is to create a safe and open environment so that your participants feel comfortable to speak freely and honestly to the group.
4. Prepare a discussion guide. Carefully plan the questions you will be asking. You must take great care that a question is not worded in a way that will "lead the witness."

Still, a good plan isn't worth a lick if you have a poor facilitator leading the discussion. If you want to learn how to be a rock star facilitator, I recommend reading *The Secrets of Facilitation* by Michael Wilkinson.

Ethnography

While interviews and focus groups are excellent methods for collecting qualitative data, there's always a possibility that people will mask their true feelings or at least downplay the significance of a response. To remove any possibility of this happening, we turn to the third and final qualitative method I want to share with you: ethnographic research.

This is a method of research in which often the participants don't know they're part of a study. That's because you observe them "in the wild." For example, a kitchen remodeler may watch how people use their kitchens while they cook, making note of problems they encounter in their existing layout, so that he or she can incorporate solutions in his designs.

A website developer can use eye-tracking and mouse-tracking tools to "watch" how website visitors interact with the website he or she has built and make improvements based on the results.

The point is to observe rather than interact. Of course, the occasional conversational question is okay. For instance, the kitchen remodeler could say, "Why do you keep your condiments in that cabinet?" without significantly influencing the study. Even so, zero interaction is preferable.

In summary, qualitative research nicely compliments quantitative methods. When used in tandem, they enable you to see the whole story of not only what people are thinking and feeling, but why it is so. As Albert Einstein once said, "Not everything that can be counted counts, and not everything that counts can be counted." For those things that matter, but cannot be counted, qualitative methods provide the in-depth insight to ensure your questions are answered.

FOUR
BUILDING YOUR INFORMATION ROAD MAP

THE SINGLE BIGGEST MISTAKE A MARKETER CAN MAKE is to forgo a written plan. And I'm not just talking about a research plan. I mean *any* plan. Most of the time, it's because—since you are the person who will execute it—you figure it's a waste of time. After all, it's all in your head anyway, right?

The importance of having a written plan cannot be overstated. It's your road map to achieving your goal. Without it, you're setting yourself up to fail. You must put yourself through the necessary steps of discovery in order to succeed.

With regard to research, a plan helps you visualize and identify precisely what methods you should use to get the answers you want to find. This needn't be a complex thesis with chapters and an index. A one-page document should suffice.

Writing the research plan consists of three steps:

Step One: State the Problem and Objectives

Your problem statement articulates what it is you hope to learn. For example, a kitchen remodeler may want to better understand the role the husband plays in the sales process. So two objectives could be the following:

1. Determine how much influence the husband has on the selections being made (e.g., cabinets, appliances, and so on)

2. Determine what role brand name plays in his decision-making process.

Step Two: Define Who Is Going to Participate

This could be past clients, existing clients, lost clients, newsletter subscribers, strangers off the street, and on and on. Naturally, your pool of participants depends largely on what you hope to learn.

Step 3: Define the Methods to Conduct the Research

This is influenced by the results of steps one and two. Look at each of your objectives and determine which of the various qual and quant methods are best suited to get the answers you need. Use a table to help organize your thoughts.

	Determine influence the husband has on the selections being made	Determine what role brand name plays in his decision
Survey Past Clients (quant)		X
1:1's Past Clients (qual)	X	X
Ethnographic— go on sales calls	X	

In conclusion, it matters not the size of your company. If you have a business, you must make the collection of market data a high priority. Without it, you are relying on hunches, guesswork, and luck.

In most cases, it's not necessary to hire an agency to conduct intensive market research on your behalf. DIY research for smaller companies is just fine. It's better than moving forward with no information at all. Like Gordon Gekko said, "There's nothing more valuable than information." The more you have, the better your ability to make sound decisions that will guide you down the path to success.

[SECTION TWO]

BECOMING THE LOBSTER

The hardest choices require the strongest wills.

—Thanos, *Avengers: Infinity War*

FIVE
THE PURE, ABSOLUTE POWER OF POSITIONING

FROM IRON MAN TO SPIDER-MAN, FROM LOKI TO RONAN, the Marvel Cinematic Universe (MCU) has delivered some remarkable superheroes and some equally memorable supervillains. But none are as powerful, or as frightening, as Thanos, the Mad Titan—a massive being with great strength.

I mention Thanos because he is not unlike some of the companies with which you may compete, with their big marketing budgets, sales teams, and bulk-buying power. It can be frustrating, to say the least. You're every bit as good, if not better, than them, and yet you're on an uneven playing field. How can you, the mere mortal, compete with those resources?

Well, for all his size and strength, even Thanos isn't all-powerful. So whether your largest competitor is an established local business or a multinational giant, all is not lost. The film *Avengers: Infinity War* has given us the blueprint for defeating a competitor of any size, and as you must have deduced by the title of this chapter, it's through positioning.

Positioning is the single most powerful marketing tool you have at your disposal. It is the great equalizer. Having a powerful, well-crafted position can empower even the smallest local business to go toe-to-toe with companies of any size—and win.

So how do you go toe-to-toe with a titan? Well, in the MCU there exist the six Infinity Stones—extremely powerful gems that, when united, give the bearer limitless power. Similarly, in our marketing universe exist the six Positioning Stones. And just like in the MCU, when these stones are united, you will achieve limitless, unstoppable power.

In this section, we'll look at each of the six Positioning Stones in detail, and I'll give you the tools you need to develop your invincible position in the market.

But before we can dive into the unique power of the individual Positioning Stones, you need to have a clear understanding of what positioning is and how it differs from your position in the market. Your position is the distinct place your brand holds—relative to competing brands—in the mind of the customer. Let me say that again: your position exists *in the mind* of the customer. Your position is, in many ways, the perceptions, attitudes, and emotions your customers feel about your brand.

This means you don't own your position. It belongs to everyone else.

Now, that may seem like a laughable assertion meant to romanticize what marketers do, but consider this: if McDonald's opened a location near you, and said *this* location is a fine-dining restaurant, would you accept that?

Probably not.

But what if they added tablecloths, a maître d', and valet parking? Would that be enough to get you to make a reservation at McDonald's for your twenty-fifth wedding anniversary?

Not, I suspect, if you want to make it to year twenty-six.

You see, if McDonald's truly *owned* its position, then it could decide at any time to change it, and the marketplace would accept that change.

But they don't. No brand on earth does, no matter how large.

The best a brand—*any brand*—can do, is try to *influence* its position.

And *that* is positioning. Whereas your position is the distinct place your brand holds in the mind of the customer, positioning is *the process of influencing* the place that your brand holds in the mind of the customer.

To better understand the pure, undeniable power of positioning, let's look at a real-world example. When you think of Jaguar, what thoughts and emotions come to mind? Most people I've asked say words like *prestigious*, *expensive*, *classy*, *pretentious*, *extravagant*, and *elitist*, just to name a few. Do you agree with some or all of these descriptors?

Would you also agree that it is reasonable to expect to pay $70,000 for a Jaguar? (Note, I'm not asking if you *would* pay that much, just if it's a reasonable expectation.)

Now let's contrast Jaguar with Hyundai. What feelings and emotions does this brand conjure up? To this question, I will often hear words like *economical*, *affordable*, *practical*, *sensible*, *cheap*, *entry-level*, and so on.

So with that in mind, would you consider $70,000 a reasonable price to pay for a Hyundai?

What if I told you that I walked onto a Hyundai lot yesterday and saw an elegant, black luxury sedan that looked like it belonged in the next James Bond film. Would you then consider spending $70,000 on a Hyundai?

Okay, how about this: what if you won a raffle that allowed you to select any car with a $70,000 price tag, and you could drive it off any lot you choose, absolutely free? Surely now you would consider my Bond-like Hyundai, wouldn't you?

No. Probably not. With a world of Porsches, Mercedes-Benzes, Jaguars, BMWs, and Cadillacs, driving off with a Hyundai just doesn't seem like a good choice, regardless of its quality.

Hyundai's position in your mind simply will not allow you to accept the comparison to one of these luxury brands. In fact, Hyundai's position is so deeply rooted that a character in the 1992 film *Glengarry Glen Ross* mentions it explicitly. Blake, a highly successful salesman played by Alec Baldwin, is sent by the firm's owners to motivate (more or less) the underperforming sales team. The sales team, in return, defends their lack of sales as a result of poor-quality leads.

"The leads are weak," they argue. Blake, in a curse-punctuated exchange, tells the team that *they*, not the leads, are the weak elements, and that the proof is in their rides. Blake says, "You drove a *Hyundai* to get here tonight, I drove an $80,000 BMW."

If your brand's position is so firmly planted in the collective conscious that it makes it into a film, pat yourself on the back, pop the champagne, and congratulate yourself for a job well done.

I would understand if you're thinking, "But, Mark, that scene was really bad for Hyundai." After all, Blake's intent was to insult and demean the salesmen. True. But in doing so, he is simply stating the two brands positions in the market: Hyundai is the practical, affordable, economy car that anyone can own, regardless of social status, whereas BMW is for the highly successful businessman with extravagant taste and disposable income.

This isn't a bad thing. It is precisely the position Hyundai has worked hard to achieve. Just think: *even a bad salesman can afford a Hyundai.*

Okay, maybe it's not the best tagline. But you get the point.

Unfortunately for Hyundai, they weren't satisfied with a job well done. The luxury Hyundai scenario I described earlier isn't a fiction I fabricated to prove a point. Hyundai did, in fact, create a luxury car: the Equus, a $70,000 full-sized luxury sedan. Have you heard of it? If you haven't, it doesn't much matter, because it doesn't exist anymore. (Can you guess why?)

As you can see, it makes no difference how big you are or how much money you have. The laws of positioning apply to brands of all sizes. You can't flip a switch and suddenly decide to move your brand to another position in the market on a whim. And you most certainly can't hold two different positions at the same time, which is what Hyundai tried to do. You need to think of your position as a physical place upon which you stand; and as you know, you can't be in two places at once. It's basic physics.

One big reason why the Equus was doomed from the start was that Hyundai didn't take into consideration the motivations and attitudes of the Equus's target market (people willing and able to spend $70k on a car). This is very different from Hyundai's existing target, people who typically spend $18,000 to $20,000 on a car. Had they done so, they would have quickly discovered the one big, glaring motivation that people who spend $70,000 on a car share that Hyundai is not equipped to satisfy: they want other people to *know* they spent $70,000 on a car! Driving around town with the Hyundai emblem on the hood simply cannot satisfy this need.

Hyundai finally figured it out and discontinued the Equus in 2016.

But they didn't give up. They got smart.

They accepted the fact that even Goliath companies can't break the laws of positioning, and did the only thing a company in their position could do; they started a new company.

Genesis Motor, LLC, (commonly referred to simply as Genesis) is a luxury vehicle manufacturer wholly owned by Hyundai Motor Group. The company logo (a crest bearing the Genesis name with flying wings on either side) looks remarkably similar to the Bentley logo. And that discontinued luxury car, the Equus, is now called the Genesis G90. Apart from the emblem on its hood, the two models look almost identical. I suspect not much has changed under the hood, either.

The new company makes no mention of its parent company anywhere. Not on its website. Not on its brochures. You would have no way of knowing this company was part of the Hyundai Motor Group without doing some digging on your own.

Consider the implications. A previously nonexistent brand has a better chance of competing with established luxury brands than does a well-known brand which holds a different position in the minds of consumers. This truly demonstrates the undeniable power of positioning.

And, if you were wondering: *US News and World Report* ranked Genesis the #3 Best Luxury Vehicle Brand for 2020.

SIX
THE SIX STONES OF POSITIONING

IN THE MCU, THANOS WORE SOMETHING CALLED THE Infinity Gauntlet, which contained six slots to house each of the six Infinity Stones. (A gauntlet, if you're not familiar, is an armored glove worn by soldiers and knights during combat.) Marketers don't ride into battle with a gauntlet. Instead, we wield a positioning statement, which also has six slots in which to insert each of the six Positioning Stones. By the end of this section, you will have found all six of your stones, completed your positioning statement, and be prepared to dominate your market.

The positioning statement is one of three critical *statements* every business should have. The other two are the vision statement and the mission statement. Most small businesses have at least one. Usually, it's the mission statement. But all three are critical to building a successful business.

Here's why. The mission statement focuses on today and what the company *does*. The mission describes the reason the company exists. For example, Google's mission is "to organize the world's information and make it universally accessible and useful."

A vision statement is more ambitious. It focuses on tomorrow and on what the company *aspires to be*. The best vision statements sound almost mystical. Nike's vision is "to bring inspiration and innovation to every athlete* in the world. (*If you have a body, you are an athlete.)"

This is one of the greatest vision statements I have ever read. For one thing, I've never seen anyone use an asterisk and a footnote in a vision statement. But beyond that, I love how their vision includes getting every human being on the planet to consider themselves an athlete, regardless of what shape they are in. What a remarkable, altruistic vision.

Still, vision statements needn't be a virtually unachievable goal like Nike's. Although there *is* something to be said for being part of an organization that sets the bar so high that it would take a god to achieve. That said, the purpose of the vision statement, ultimately, is to guide the company's direction for years to come. That seems like a pretty important document for a company to have, wouldn't you agree?

Where the mission is *why* you exist, and the vision is *where* you are going, the positioning statement is *how* you will do it. More specifically, it's how you do it in a way that no one else can.

But the positioning statement is unique in that, unlike the vision and mission, it's possible for a company to have more than one positioning statement.

Let me rephrase that: all companies should have one *brand*-positioning statement, but some may need multiple product-positioning statements.

Whether or not you need to venture into the complexities of product-positioning statements will depend on whether your products and services vary to the degree that they appeal to different target audiences or face different competitors.

For example, if a builder offers kitchen remodeling, bathroom remodeling, basement remodeling, and additions, would it make sense for him to create a positioning statement for each? Maybe, but probably not.

However, if the builder offers new-home construction, remodeling, and handyman services, then it may be necessary to "de-average" himself and have four positioning statements (the brand-positioning statement and three service-positioning statements) since the three services will be competing against very different companies and may even target different customers.

Truth be told, in a scenario like this, it's not uncommon for the business owner to refer to the services as *divisions* of the company. (e.g., my handyman division, my remodeling division, and so on) This is a good litmus test. If you consider your products or services to be different divisions of your company, you probably need product-positioning statements. If not, a single brand-positioning statement will suffice.

It's important to remember, however, that any product-positioning statements you create are subservient to the brand's overarching umbrella position. Just as the Hyundai case study revealed, a brand can't hold one position and have its products hold another.

Regardless of whether you need product-positioning statements or not, everyone must start with their company's brand-position statement. So keep that in mind as we work through this section.

As I said, the positioning statement houses the six Positioning Stones. These stones are

1. Target—your ideal customer;
2. Unmet Need—the problem your product or service solves;
3. Competitive Set—who or what you are competing with;
4. Point of Difference—what makes you different from the competition;
5. Reasons to Believe—the proof that supports your point of difference; and
6. Brand Personality—your distinctive character.

The first three stones, Target, Unmet Need, and Competitive Set, are what I call the Outward Stones, as they pertain to elements that exist outside of your company. The last three stones, Point of Difference, Reasons to Believe, and Brand Personality, are the Inward Stones because they pertain to elements that exist within your company.

The basic positioning statement looks like this:

For [TARGET] who [UNMET NEED], [COMPANY, PRODUCT, OR SERVICE] is the [COMPETITIVE SET] that [POINT OF DIFFERENCE] because [REASON TO BELIEVE 1], and [REASON TO BELIEVE 2]. We convey this by being [BRAND PERSONALITY].

I know it doesn't look like much now. But once we find your stones and place them in their respective slots, your positioning statement will become an elegant weapon that will lead your company to limitless victories.

SEVEN
STONE ONE: TARGET

WHO IS YOUR TARGET MARKET? THIS IS ONE OF THE FIRST questions I ask, and half the time I get the *worst* possible answer: "My target is anyone who needs [thing I offer] in my service area."

Everyone cannot be your target market.

Ever.

I'm sorry.

Imagine if you were to ask the directors of marketing for Hyundai and Jaguar who their target was, and both responded, "Anyone in the United States who needs a car."

Do you see how wrong that is?

Seriously, if corporations with marketing budgets greater than the GDP of a small country can't get away with it, what makes you think you can?

You must accept the fact that you cannot be all things to all people. If you try, then you're nothing to nobody. Our goal for this chapter is to clearly identify your target of one. Who is your bullseye?

For some, this is the most difficult stone to create. I have *never* run a class that didn't have at least one person dig their heels in and fight me tooth and nail on this stone.

"I have more than one target." This is the song of the stubborn. When I hear this chorus, I often wish I could have Col. Jessup walk into the room and exclaim, "You want more than one target? *You can't handle more than one target*!"

There are many reasons why you must focus on a single target, but the biggest is that you can't *afford* to have more than one target.

Very few small businesses can. A marketing budget doesn't enjoy economies of scale. If you have two targets, your budget is effectively cut in half.

So while you're spending half of your budget trying to reach target A, your competitors are spending 100 percent of their budgets on that same target. (And it should go without saying, but if you're that guy who's also trying to reach targets C, D, and E, then good luck. I'll be praying for you.)

Most who challenge me on this do so out of fear. I understand. It seems like you're drastically cutting the number of potential customers in your service area, and that feels like a big mistake. But this is head trash. Having a target of one doesn't mean you can't *sell* to people outside of your defined target. All it means is that you are focusing your marketing efforts on reaching your ideal customer.

Consider Apple. Do you think their target is women between the ages of eighty-five and a hundred? No. However, do you think that they would sell an iPhone to a ninety-two-year-old woman? Of course they would.

If you are still of the mind that you require more than one target, that is your choice. I will never try to bend the unbendable. Just understand that you will have to create a separate positioning statement for each of your targets, and you will have less money to spend as you try to reach each one of them.

There are two elements that define the first stone. They are demographics and psychographics.

Demographics is the easiest to define. These are the measurable dry facts that you will use to identify your target customer. This includes things like age, race, sex, religion, marital status, family size, ethnicity, education, income, and so on.

Psychographics are more difficult to identify. They focus on the underlying interests, activities, values, opinions, aspirations, and other psychological factors that motivate your target customer.

One method for working through this process is to look back at past customers. Which ones were the best to work with? Did you ever have the perfect customer, one you wish you could clone? Have there been more than one? What traits do they have in common? Make sure to list all the demographic and psychographic factors you can think of.

Take some time, now, to brainstorm these factors.

When you're done, review the list and look for holes. Is it comprehensive? What else do you wish you knew? Go back to your research and find out. What questions would you ask? Would you use qual or quant?

Take your time and be clear. There's a bit of an art to this process. If your result is too broad, you've got more work to do. If it's too narrow, you'll go out of business.

As I said, you cannot be all things to all people. By focusing on a target of one, you can refine your message to the point at which you become the clear and obvious choice for the people that you consider to be your ideal customer. We'll discuss this is great detail in Section Three: "Finding the Lobster Lovers."

EIGHT
STONE TWO: UNMET NEED

NOW THAT YOU HAVE A CLEAR PICTURE OF WHO YOUR target customer is, you can work to identify his or her unmet need. The unmet need is the problem that your brand promises to solve for the customer. Some refer to this stone as the customer's pain, but this categorization can be misleading. After all, if I'm looking for a belt to match the new shoes I bought, I wouldn't say I'm feeling *pain*. I do, however, have a need that is yet to be met, which is why I prefer to call this stone the Unmet Need.

On that note, let's stay with the belt and shoes dilemma for a moment. Do you know what my unmet need is in this scenario?

If you said, "You need a belt that matches your shoes," you would be partially correct. Needing a belt that matches my shoes would satisfy my *functional* need. But there are two types of unmet needs: functional and emotional. Can you think of what emotional needs I may have? Take a moment to consider the possibilities before reading on.

Perhaps it's a fear of being ridiculed by my peers (i.e., can you believe he thinks a brown belt goes with that outfit?). Or maybe it's my desire to be perceived as a stylish trendsetter.

All unmet needs have a functional and emotional component—*all unmet needs.* As you work to develop the unmet need that your brand solves for your target, I want you to consider both of them. And don't hold back. Brainstorm any and all possible needs, regardless of whether you can solve them.

To help you discover your target's emotional need, consider this list of words that are commonly associated with emotional needs:

- fear
- anger
- relief
- freedom
- confidence
- pride
- peace of mind
- approval
- envy
- acceptance
- admiration

Once you've completed the brainstorming exercise, you need to find the winner. But how do you know when you've got it? You run it through the *I Wish I Could* test. This means simply prefacing the unmet need with the phrase *I Wish I Could*, and then determining if it's something someone would realistically think to themselves.

For example, I once worked with Marty, the marketing manager of a software-as-a-service company (SaaS). Marty concluded that his target's unmet need was that she needed to improve her workflow efficiency. I thought Marty was on the right track, but he wasn't there yet. To prove it, we applied the test. In this case, the test yielded the statement, "I wish I could improve my workflow efficiency."

I think it's safe to say that, since the dawn of man, this is not a phrase that anyone has ever said in earnest.

So what do you do now? You dig deeper. You must get to the root of the unmet need. And we do this by using the Five Whys technique.

This is a repetitive questioning exercise originally developed by Sakichi Toyoda and was used in the Toyota Production System (TPS). Put simply, you ask a scenario *why*. Each answer forms the basis of the next why question. This pattern continues until you've arrived at the root cause. It needn't be repeated five times. It may take only four *whys* to get to the root; it may take seven or more.

Continuing our example, let's see how the Five Whys technique helped Marty discover the target's emotional unmet need.

Marty: You must improve your workflow efficiency.

Me: *Why?*

Marty: So that you can get your work done faster.

Me: *Why would I want that?*

Marty: So that you can leave the office before rush hour.

Me: *Why does that matter?*

Marty: So that you get home earlier.

This example shows how powerful the Five Whys technique can be. But for the technique to truly work, you need to keep pushing the envelope. When you think you've got it, run it through the test again. Here, we ended on, "I wish I could get home earlier." That certainly works. I've said that myself plenty of times.

And yet, you need to go as deep as possible. Can we push harder? Can we ask *why* again? In this case, Marty thought we had gotten to the root, but I pushed him. "*Why would I want to get home earlier?*" I asked.

That's when we got to the real root. "So you don't miss your kid's soccer game."

As you can see, the *I Wish I Could* test and the Five Whys technique, when used diligently in concert, can help you drill deep into the mind of your target and discover the true emotional need.

NINE
STONE THREE: COMPETITIVE SET

THE FINAL OUTWARD STONE IS THE COMPETITIVE SET. It's generally the easiest to find. This is where you state *what* you are, where you do it, and, subsequently, with whom your company competes. Put simply, it's the sandbox you play in.

Gatorade's competitive set, for example, would be "a sports-themed beverage and food product manufacturer." This then means that any other companies that manufacture sports-themed beverages and food would compete with Gatorade. As you can see, how you define what you are directly affects with whom you compete.

That being said, you don't necessarily have to identify yourself in such a straightforward way. An advanced strategy for companies that are in a saturated market is to get creative with this stone.

To illustrate, let's look at Charmin's competitive set. One might say that Charmin is an American brand of bathroom tissue paper. This would mean that Charmin's competitors are other bathroom tissue brands such as Scott, Cottonelle, Quilted, and Angel Soft.

But what if we said, instead, that Charmin is the ultimate Halloween prank accessory? Now its competitors would be eggs, plastic cling wrap, and shaving cream. See how that works?

For a more realistic example, consider a company that builds custom playsets and treehouses. Its out-of-the-box stone would probably be "a custom outdoor play area builder," and, as such, it would compete with other companies that build and install playsets and treehouses.

But what if we said this company is an outdoor fun and adventure provider? Well, now it competes with theme parks, recreation centers, campgrounds, and so on. Positioning themselves as a summer-long alternative to a one-day trip could be just the ticket to dominating their market.

Or consider a contractor that specializes in aging-in-place remodeling (this is, remodeling that focuses on altering the home so that people can live in it safely, independently, and comfortably, regardless of age). This company probably thinks it is competing with other remodelers, and would define itself as a residential remodeler that specializes in aging in place. But this could be a mistake, because the target market may not even know that aging-in-place remodeling is an option.

If they, instead, define themselves as a housing provider for seniors, their competition now becomes nursing homes, assisted-living facilities, and even real estate agents (because moving to a smaller one-story rancher is also an option).

So before you quickly jot down the dictionary definition of what you do, I challenge you to dig deep and brainstorm other ways to look at what you offer. You may be surprised to find whom you're actually competing against.

TEN
STONE FOUR: POINT OF DIFFERENCE

WE NOW MOVE ON TO THE INWARD STONES. THESE ARE the Positioning Stones that pertain to elements that exist *within* your company. The first inward stone, however, is the most valuable of all six Positioning Stones. That's because it is at the heart of the entire Positioning Statement. In fact, it has *the potential* to be the most powerful stone you have. The Point of Difference stone is, in a word, your *why*. Why should the prospect choose you?

The strongest POD stones meet three criteria: your target wants it, none of your competitors can claim it, and you can prove it.

Some have called this stone your Unique Selling Proposition, or USP. I, however, have never liked that term. I think it clouds the mind and tempts you to come up with concepts that fit neatly into an elevator pitch. I don't want you thinking in terms of making a sales pitch to a prospect. I want you focusing solely on how you help the client in a way that no one else can.

Oftentimes, I meet with clients who believe they have this stone firmly in their grasp. But it turns out to be nothing more than a fake, or a *fugazi*, as Donnie Brasco so eloquently put it in the movie of the same name. Here are a dozen fugazi stones I've encountered in just the past month:

- We pride ourselves on providing unmatched service.
- Family-owned since 1978.

- We offer the highest quality craftsmanship.
- We offer small class sizes.
- We take pride in our proven ability to listen to your needs.
- We guarantee your satisfaction.
- Our commitment is to quality.
- We hire only highly trained experts and only work with state-of-the-art tools.
- We take pride in our work, and we love what we do.
- Our team can bring you the absolute best management skills.
- Our streamlined processes and experienced team ensure that your work gets done swiftly.

Do you see how these are fakes? Check each statement against the three criteria (want it, claim it, prove it), and it's clear. Can none of your competitors *claim* to be committed to quality? Can you *prove* that you offer a level of service that cannot be matched?

Besides not meeting the criteria of a genuine Point of Difference, many of these fugazi stones are useless platitudes. Even if you could provide indisputable proof that one of them were true, like providing unmatched service (really?), your target has heard it so many times that it's just white noise. It no longer carries any weight.

Now, you may be thinking, *But, Mark, what's wrong with "Family-owned since 1978?" That one meets all three criteria!* I would argue that, besides being a platitude, it only meets two of the three. While it may be true that none of your competitors were founded in the year 1978, I promise your target isn't walking around thinking, *I need to find a company that was founded in 1978.*

No, the spirit of this claim is to tout longevity and experience. And odds are you have a competitor that can claim the same. "Celebrating twenty-five years of service" has the same effect, and that company would have been founded in 1995, a full seventeen years after yours. Do you think your target would ever take the time to do the math? And do you think it would even matter to them if they did?

Don't get me wrong. I'm not suggesting that years of experience isn't important. I'm merely pointing out that it doesn't qualify as your point of difference. It may, however, work as the fifth stone: Reasons to Believe.

The truth is that the fourth and fifth stones can be a bit tricky. It's not uncommon to misidentify a Point of Difference as a Reason to Believe, or vice versa. You'll see what I mean when we talk about the fifth stone, in the next chapter.

Let's get back to identifying your Point of Difference. As I've shown, if your claim doesn't meet all three criteria, it's a weak stone. The most powerful Points of Difference are extremely rare. By definition, only one of its kind will exist in your entire market.

An example of a powerful stone, a one-of-a-kind in the market, would be, "We are the only authorized supplier of product X in the state of Georgia." This means that if I want to purchase product X, I must either come to you or leave the state of Georgia to buy it. That's a powerful thing, wouldn't you agree?

Another example would be laying claim to something proprietary, like software, tools, processes, etc. These are extremely powerful Point of Difference stones because, again, no one else can claim them. Imagine there are two competing daycare centers, and one could say, "Our custom-built app let's you log in anytime and see a live video stream of your child." They would be well on their way to crushing the competition.

Obviously, these are difficult stones to come by. You can't just snap your fingers and be the exclusive supplier of a product, or have some custom-built app. But such is the way to limitless power. If it were easy, everyone would be doing it.

There is, however, a Point of Difference that is (relatively speaking) easier to claim and which still packs a powerful punch. It's specialization. If your brand focuses on a specific niche, then you have a great way to differentiate yourself from the competition.

Okay, let's uncover your Point of Difference stone. The goal is to find *the most powerful* Point of Difference you offer, so even if you think you already know it, don't skip this part. There may be a stronger stone hidden right under your nose. Here are four exercises that can help you find it:

1. Make a list of all your features—features being surface statements about what your product or service can do. It's fact-based stuff, like material quality, size, longevity, compatibility, and so on.
2. Make a list of all your benefits—benefits being the impact a feature has on your customer, including their feelings and emotions.
3. Answer the question, "What do I do best?" List anything and everything that comes to mind, no matter how small. And don't be concerned at this point if it is unique to you. Just write down everything. This is brainstorming time.
4. Think backward. List all the things that can go horribly wrong if a customer makes a bad buying decision. This can help you uncover the ways that you prevent these things from happening, which, in turn, could be your Point of Difference.

Once you have all your brainstorming lists completed, it's time to start sifting through the results. You're looking for something that—*ideally*—directly addresses the Unmet Need stone you discovered earlier.

For purposes of example, we're going to use a fictional deck builder, Fluffy Decks, LLC, for the remainder of this section. Fluffy Decks has identified their target as *the stay-at-home mom in her thirties with young children*. They determined that her unmet need is "peace of mind that her kids will be safe." That unmet need ultimately drives us to identify Fluffy Deck's point of difference as: "Family health and safety is our singular focus."

Take your time and work through this exercise vigorously. It could take hours. It could take days. Don't give up on it too easily. Like I said, this is hard work. The most powerful are extremely rare.

Unfortunately, the reality is that for some of you reading this book there's nothing to find. But if you discover that your Point of Difference is either weak or nonexistent, don't panic. We'll just have to create one. And create one we will, because moving forward without a point of difference is not an option.

Companies that lack this stone are nothing more than commodities, like sugar and eggs. And what is it that all commodities have in common? They're purchased based on price. Why spend $2.39 for a carton of extra-large eggs if the store across the street has them for $0.99?

Eggs are eggs, right?

Gas is the same way. How many times have you made a U-turn to go to the gas station on the other side of the street just because their gas was $0.02 cheaper? Not even the convenience of being on the correct side of the street was enough to get you to pay extra *for the exact same thing*.

And that's the root of it. If you see two products or services as identical, then why pay extra? You can't do it. You feel cheated. If you're going to pay more, you expect more.

Remember: this stone is your *why*! It tells potential customers why they should choose you, and why they should be willing to pay more for you. Without it, the prospective client has no way to differentiate what you are offering from that of your competitor. As a result, you've given the customer no choice but to rely on the final tiebreaker available: price.

How to Create a Point of Difference Stone if You Don't Already Have One

You need to get inside your target customer's head. Find out why past customers chose you. Find out why the customer you lost chose your competitor.

The first step in creating a Point of Difference is to do research. It's time to put what you learned in Section One into action. Look long and hard at the unmet need stone and explore ways you can deliver a solution to that need in a way no one else can.

You may have to make some hard choices. You may even have to change a core element of your business in order to set yourself apart from your competition.

Don't be scared. Trust your research and trust your gut.

A Solution for Your Consideration

If you're struggling with creating a point of difference, I suggest you consider the aforementioned niche solution. Focusing on a niche can give you a decisive advantage over your competition.

Whenever I broach this subject with a client, I usually get a great deal of pushback. "I don't want to lose customers," they say. I understand the fear. Why would you intentionally alienate 40, 50, even 75 percent of the prospects in your service area?

It may seem counterintuitive, but narrowing your focus broadens your appeal.

Let me prove it to you. Which of the following marketing agencies do you think Fluffy Decks should hire?

Agency A: We're a full-service marketing agency that helps B2B and B2C businesses reach more customers through compelling strategy, websites, content, video, and branding. Let us help you.

Agency B: We're more than a full-service marketing agency. We're different because we work exclusively with remodelers. We are intimately aware of the unique marketing challenges you face, and we're poised to help you overcome those challenges.

Who would you choose? (Remember: you're the owner of Fluffy Decks, a remodeling company.) Admittedly, both companies sound good, but Agency B is the obvious choice if you're a remodeler. After all, they only work with remodelers, so they "get" you.

The St. Louis-based law firm Cordell & Cordell is a great example of the power of niching your market. Founded in 1990 as a general practice firm, they began noticing that the majority of their clients were men. Says cofounder Joseph Cordell, "During the course of that experience, I couldn't help but notice the challenges consistently facing the guys side of the table when it comes to custody, maintenance issues, and accusations of domestic violence. I found in waging those fights that I enjoyed it more. So we proclaimed ourselves as a firm that devoted itself to representing men in domestic relations matters."

Not only did the firm set itself as specialists in divorce and similar family law practice areas, (such as child custody, child support, and property division), but they also positioned themselves as *A Partner Men Can Count On*, as their tagline declares. I hear their ads on our local sports radio station, and they are, in my opinion, some of the best legal ads I have ever heard. One ad in particular niches even further, reaching out to men who have been blindsided by a sudden divorce request from their spouse—something they never saw coming.

This may seem counterintuitive, to speak to such a narrow subset of the population. But the power is irrefutable. Cordell & Cordell has grown to more than a hundred offices across the United States and has even opened an office in London.

There are four undeniable truths when it comes to niching your market.

Undeniable Truth #1 A niche business is perceived to be able to do it better than a general-purpose company. And I'm not just talking about our logic. This perception impacts both logic and emotion. It's logical to think that doing one thing over and over makes you better at it. And, emotionally, it puts your mind at ease to know that you're working with a specialist.

Here's something else to consider. Using the Fluffy Decks example again, imagine you call both agencies above, and you find out Agency A (who works with all B2B and B2C businesses) charges $200 per hour, and Agency B (who only works with remodelers) charges $325 per hour. What do you think of them now? Who do you think would do a better job of marketing for Fluffy Decks?

For most, the higher price only *strengthens* the impression that Agency B is the better choice. Which brings me to—

Undeniable Truth #2: A niche business can charge a premium for their services because they are "the expert," and experts are better at their trade than generalists could ever hope to be.

However, now that you "know" Agency B is the better choice for Fluffy Decks, does that mean Fluffy Decks should choose them? Well, that depends, doesn't it? What's at stake? If all you need is someone to do some social media posts and send out a newsletter once a month, then maybe the $200 agency is good enough. But if you've budgeted a 20 percent increase in sales for the year, and your lead flow has been falling off, then you need the best option out there to right the ship.

The truth is that whatever is at stake will play a big role in your decision. This leads us to—

Undeniable Truth #3: It can help you land better clients.

A company that has successfully carved out a niche will have set the prospect's expectations before the phone rings. That means niche companies will typically have a higher close rate than the "we-do-it all" companies, because their leads are prequalified. For small companies that don't have the time to chase bad leads, this is a huge benefit. And for larger companies, this is a great way to increase efficiency.

Of course, it's not all butterflies and daisies. By no means will the choice to pursue a niche market guarantee success, and there are certainly some pitfalls. For example, getting too niche can be disastrous. You must be sure that there's enough demand for your niche to support a growing company. So don't rush into it. Like all business decisions, it requires in-depth analysis and critical assessment. But for some, niching your market will be the strongest Point of Difference you'll be able to create—and a niche is a formidable stone indeed.

The Fourth Stone's Alter Ego

There's something special about the Fourth Positioning Stone. It's something that none of the other stones have: an alter ego. It's called the Points of Parity. The Points of Parity side of the fourth stone only rears its head in one specific circumstance: when you are not the market leader in your space, *and you want to challenge the leader for the same position.*

If you're looking to take on a market leader for the same position, read on. If not, feel free to skip to Chapter Eleven.

But before I explain the purpose and use of the Points of Parity side of the fourth stone, let's look at a tool you would use to determine if you were taking on a competitor head-on.

Perceptual mapping is a technique used to show how customers perceive competing brands in the marketplace. It's a simple yet powerful tool. Perceptual maps are two-dimension graphs in which you specify an attribute on the horizontal axis (x) and another attribute on the vertical axis (y). This forms a two-by-two grid. You then plot the brands on the grid by placing a circle on the spot along the two axis continuums in which each brand exists. This neatly packages brands into one of four quadrants. Your *direct* competitors are those that exist in your quadrant. The closer your circle is to another brand, the more directly you compete with them. Some perceptual maps use different-sized circles to indicate the size or market share of the brand.

Figure 1 shows a sample perceptual map for car brands. The two attributes being plotted are age and taste. The x-axis represents age with *Younger Demographic* on the far left and *Older Demographic* on the far right. The y-axis represents taste with *Extravagant* at the top and *Practical* at the bottom. This creates four distinct target market quadrants: 1) younger people with extravagant taste; 2) older people with extravagant taste; 3) younger people with practical taste; 4) older people with practical taste.

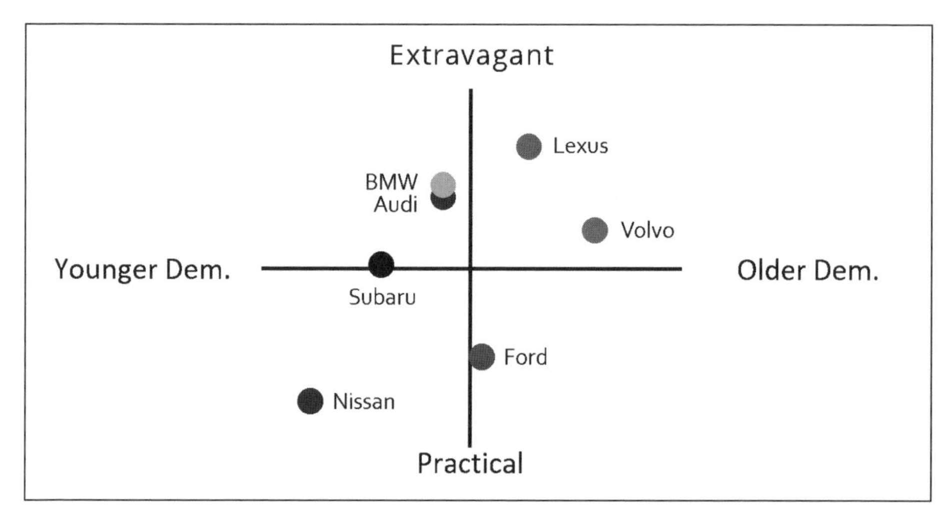

Figure 1

In the sample illustrated, you can see how this map helps visualize who you compete with, and to what extent. For example, Lexus and Volvo are both in the same quadrant—competing for the older demographic with extravagant taste. But they are far enough apart within that quadrant that you could see a path to them being able to reach their respective target markets without significant overlap.

Conversely, you can see that BMW and Audi are literally overlapping. According to this map, they are competing for the same consumer.

This scenario—BMW and Audi—is the situation in which the fourth stone's alter ego, the Points of Parity (POP), come into play. Where Points of Difference highlight what makes you unique, Points of Parity describe how you are *similar* to the market leader.

Why would you want to do that? Because you want people to see that you are just as good as the leader. It's proof that you are good enough to be included in the conversation. When used in conjunction with your Point of Difference, you can develop a formidable offensive against the market leader's position.

Seeing It in Action

Let's use Powerade as an example. They are clearly playing second fiddle to the sports drink market leader, Gatorade. Using POD and POP, you can see a path to stealing market share from Gatorade. First, we tell everyone how we're the same (Points of Parity). We have similar flavors. We are priced the same. We effectively replace water and electrolytes.

Okay, so as a consumer, I can now see that I'm getting a lot of the same things regardless of which brand I choose. That's good. Now you come at the consumer with the Point of Difference: Powerade contains fewer calories and more vitamins than Gatorade.

As you can see, the goal is to take advantage of the well-known market leader's position by showing that not only do you offer all the things you love about them, you also offer something they can't.

ELEVEN
STONE FIVE: REASONS TO BELIEVE

Me, I'm dishonest, and a dishonest man you can always trust to be dishonest. Honestly, it's the honest ones you have to watch out for.

—Jack Sparrow, Pirates of the Caribbean

WELL DONE. YOU'VE UNCOVERED YOUR POINT OF Difference, the heart of your Positioning Statement. Now it's time to sit back, shine that stone upon the world, and watch the leads come pouring in.

Not quite.

Truth be told, for all its strength, the Point of Difference stone has one major flaw: it cannot power itself. Without evidence to support it, your point of difference is nothing more than a mere stated claim. You can't just say, "trust me, it's true," and call it a day.

That's where the fifth Positioning Stone comes in. Its sole purpose is to fuel your Point of Difference. The Reasons to Believe Stone is, as the name implies, proof that your Point of Difference is true.

There are three types of Reasons to Believe:

- solution-based
- mastery-based
- approval-based

Solution-based reasons to believe are things that pertain to how your business operates. They can include products you offer, tools you use, a system or process you employ, facts about your employees, and so on. To illustrate this, let us return to our fictional deck builder, Fluffy Decks, LLC. As you may recall, their Point of Difference was, "Family health and safety is our singular focus." A solution-based Reason to Believe could be "We use vinyl decking boards on every deck we build." This is a product that they've committed to using because it keeps your family safe. Another example could be, "All decks we build must pass our proprietary Eighteen-Point Family Safety Standards test." You can see how these solution-based reasons offer proof that they make family health and safety their top priority.

Mastery-based reasons to believe demonstrate your experience. These proofs include years in business, award and recognition, accreditations you have earned, and associations of which you are a member. This is straightforward enough. But beware the temptation to go astray. Remember: this is the *Reasons to Believe Stone*. Its sole purpose is to fuel the Point of Difference. If it does not prove your POD, it is not a Positioning Stone. Fluffy Decks, LLC, could have won the remodeling industry's most prestigious exterior design award three years in a row, but receiving a design award doesn't prove that they make family health and safety their top priority. Therefore, it doesn't belong here. Stay focused on the job at hand.

Approval-based reasons to believe are arguably the most influential. They include third-party testimonials and endorsements. Face it: most people are skeptical. You're not necessarily going to be the most credible source of information if you're the one profiting from the sale. Or, at least, that's how your prospect could look at it. So being the only one tooting your horn isn't always the strongest way to go—but a testimonial from an unbiased third party who's used your product…now, that's trustworthy.

And, believe it or not (despite the fact that they are paid for), celebrity endorsements can be just as influential as client testimonials. That's because testimonials from strangers aren't as powerful as a recommendation from a friend. And a celebrity (or another well-known figure) is considered a friend. It's not naïveté. It's grounded in science. Our brains are wired to recognize people we know for self-preservation. It's how we distinguish friend from foe. If you see someone you know, and you like the person, you consider them a trustworthy friend (at least unconsciously).

One last word on approval-based reasons to believe: they don't have to be individual testimonies. They can also include statistical proofs. Here are two real-world examples of what I mean.

- Nine out of ten dentists recommend Sensodyne toothpaste.
- 95 percent of Fortune 500 companies used LinkedIn Talent Solutions in 2018.

Can you think of an example statistical proof that our fictional deck builder, Fluffy Decks, could use (assuming it were true) that supports its Point of Difference?

Remember: our goal in this chapter is to prove our Point of Difference. So if you have an approval-based Reason to Believe that speaks to your Point of Difference, you can use it. If not, save it for the testimonials page on your website.

TWELVE
STONE SIX: BRAND PERSONALITY

THE FINAL STONE IN YOUR POSITIONING STATEMENT IS Brand Personality. This is a set of emotional human characteristics that are connected to your brand. Many small businesses don't give this stone the attention it deserves, with some ignoring it altogether. But believe me when I say that this stone is just as important as all the others. If your brand doesn't exude a clear, well-defined personality then it's nothing more than a logo and a tagline—a lifeless machine.

Humans are tribal. We seek out relationships based on emotional connections. Your brand personality shapes how people will feel about you.

Have you ever met with someone and instantly connected with them? It was the person's personality with which you connected. We want people to have that same emotional connection with our brand.

This may seem like a silly, idealistic dream, but it's common for people to interact with brands as if they were people. I've personally encountered more than one person who refers to their car by a human name. "Cindy's in the shop until Tuesday," they'll say. I even have a friend who refers to his Harley-Davidson motorcycle as his wife.

Speaking of Harley-Davidson, did you know that its brand is one of the most popular tattoos in the United States? It didn't get that distinction by building the best motorcycle in the world. I mean, Samsung makes some of the best high-definition TVs on the market, and I don't see many Samsung tattoos when I walk down the boardwalk.

What makes Harley-Davidson tattoo-worthy is that people identify with its personality. Harley-Davidson is an attitude. An experience. A lifestyle.

So what should your brand personality be? Most people think it should reflect the business owner's personality, but that's not the case. Truth be told, the strongest brands have a personality that mirrors that of their target customer. Why? Because we are drawn to people who are like us. We want to hang out with people who have the same values, beliefs, and virtues as we do.

Consider Harley-Davidson's brand personality—I am a rebel, fixated on freedom. I am a masculine, flag-waving patriot who will not conform to mainstream values.

Now, think about Harley-Davidson's target market. Sensing some alignment there?

So how do you define your brand personality? Identify the personality traits of your target. Answer questions like these:

- Who is my existing customer?
- What does he or she relate to?
- How does he or she dress?
- How does he or she communicate with her friends? With family? With colleagues?
- What type of humor does he or she like? Sarcastic and dark? Self-deprecating? Deadpan? Highbrow? Quirky?
- What does he or she like to do for fun? Would the customer rather go hiking or stay in and watch a movie?

Answering these types of questions will help you determine if your brand is "acting" the way it should in order to best connect with your target customer.

Then imagine your brand was a person and describe it as such.

Our fictional company, Fluffy Decks, would define their brand personality as a sincere, kind, thoughtful, nurturing, and caring company, with a strong belief in family values. To help you define yours, I've included a list of personality traits in Appendix A.

An Audit May Be in Order

More than likely, your brand personality already exists in the minds of others. So it may be worth testing to see how you are perceived. If you have employees, that's a great place to start. Visit BeTheLobster.com/personality-worksheet to download the Brand Personality Worksheet. Hand it out to your employees and have them plot how they perceive your company.

Every sheet should come back identical. If they vary, you have work to do.

EXERCISE: THIS IS US

Brand personality is all about emotion, and a visual aid is a powerful way to convey the emotion of your brand. Consider the two photo montages on the next page. If each represented the personality of a company, you could see how drastically different your experience with these two companies would be.

For the *This is Us* exercise, you should go out on the town and take pictures of things that convey your brand personality. If you have a team, pair them up and give them a couple of hours to do the same. Then come back together and share the slideshows.

You could even take the results and create a montage of your own, and include it in your new employee onboarding process. Imagine the power of showing these images to new hires and telling them, "This is who we are, and we expect you to emulate this at all times."

\

THIRTEEN
PUTTING IT ALL TOGETHER

CONGRATULATIONS! IT WASN'T EASY, BUT YOU'VE DONE it. You have collected all six Positioning Stones and are now ready to insert them into your Positioning Statement template. Here is the completed Positioning Statement for our fictional deck builder, Fluffy Decks, LLC.

> For THE STAY-AT-HOME MOM IN HER THIRTIES WITH YOUNG CHILDREN who WANTS PEACE OF MIND THAT HER KIDS WILL ALWAYS BE SAFE, FLUFFY DECKS IS THE PREMIER FAMILY-OWNED DECK BUILDER that MAKES FAMILY HEALTH AND SAFETY ITS TOP PRIORITY because WE HAVE A "NO-EXPOSED WOOD" POLICY ON EVERY DECK WE BUILD AND ALL DECKS MUST PASS THE ADI EIGHTEEN-POINT FAMILY SAFETY STANDARDS TEST. We convey this by being A SINCERE, KIND, THOUGHTFUL, NURTURING, AND CARING COMPANY WITH A STRONG BELIEF IN FAMILY VALUES.

You can see now how this statement clearly defines where this company fits in the competitive landscape, and why no one else will be able to compete with them for their target customer.

Earlier in this book, I mentioned that, for some companies, your competitive landscape may be such that you may need to de-average your business in order to compete at the service-specific level of your competition. This is especially the case if your business has divisions of services. If this is you, then as Vizzini from *The Princess Bride* would say, "You must go back to the beginning." Return to Chapter Seven and create positioning statements for each. The process is exactly the same, with one exception: *you do not create the sixth stone again*. Your brand personality stone applies to the entire company. It is ill-advised to attempt to do otherwise.

It should be obvious why that's the case, but to illustrate my point, let's look at Apple. I would define its brand personality as being a young, hip, trendy, easygoing, casual brand that strives for simplicity. Imagine for a moment that Apple launched a new product, the iGizmo, and they tried to give this product a different personality, one more like that of Harley-Davidson—a masculine, United States flag-waving rebel.

That is an incredibly difficult sell. Even if you *could* pull it off, you'd ultimately end up weakening the parent brand personality. At best, you would confuse the marketplace and probably drive away some of your core, brand-loyal users who feel you are no longer the brand with which they connected years ago.

So I strongly recommend you don't change your personality stone, ever.

If you *are* in a situation where you need multiple positioning statements, it may help to have a Master Positioning Table that lists the divisions, identifies their roles within your company, and defines their stones. It's a good "at-a-glance" view that can help new employees and outsourced marketers alike understand why you offer the services that you do and how they fit into the company as a whole.

The sample positioning table on the next page shows what it could look like if Fluffy Decks were to have a deck division, a basement remodeling division, and a kitchen & bath remodeling division. The "role" line serves to give a descriptive explanation of how that division fits into your offering mix.

MASTER POSITIONING TABLE

	*COMPANY	DECKS	BASEMENTS	KITCHEN & BATH
ROLE	The Umbrella	The Crown Jewel	Le Créneau	The Mother Ship
TARGET	Affluent married women w/ kids that puts family 1st	Stay-at-home mom in her 30s with young children	Affluent executive dad in his 40s that loves sports	Social woman, 40s-50s with older kids, likes to entertain
UNMET NEED	Wants peace of mind that they will always be safe	Wants peace of mind that they will always be safe	The kids rule the roost and he longs for a sanctuary of his own.	Wants to be the envy of her friends and be the center of her social network
POD		Makes family health and safety its top priority.		
RTB1		we have a "no-exposed wood" policy on every deck we build		
RTB2		all decks must pass the ADI 18-point family safety standards test		
Brand Personality	A SINCERE, KIND, THOUGHTFUL, NURTURING, AND CARING COMPANY WITH A STRONG BELIEF IN FAMILY VALUES			

For Fluffy Decks, the Deck division is the crown jewel—what the business was built on. Basements are Le Créneau (French for *the niche*), because it addresses the needs of the otherwise ignored dad. The Kitchen & Bath division is the Mother Ship, bringing in the highest-revenue projects.

EXERCISE:

Create the fourth and fifth stones for their respective columns and complete the table.

You can download a blank template by visiting BeTheLobster.com/positioning-table

FOURTEEN
PRICING STRATEGY

IT SURPRISES ME HOW MANY PEOPLE DON'T THINK OF pricing strategy as a function of marketing. For the vast majority of small businesses, sell price is something that the business owner decides. He looks at the COGS (cost of goods sold) associated with the delivery of the service and applies some arbitrary markup.

The problem with this "cost-plus" approach is that it ignores your image and the value you bring to your clients. Unless you've set your point of difference as "the lowest cost provider of [service]," this method should be avoided. As was illustrated by the Hyundai case study in Chapter Five, price is directly connected to how you are positioned in the market, and as such should not be based *solely* on how much it costs you to deliver your services.

Consider the inverse scenario: imagine Jaguar discovered a new, innovative way to build the exact same car at a fraction of the cost. If their approach was to simply apply a standard markup to the COGS, then that $80,000 model vehicle would now receive a $22,000 MSRP.

What do you think that would do to their positioning? After all, if a luxury vehicle isn't expensive, is it really a luxury?

I've seen this happen with high-end remodeling firms that hire a consultant to implement Lean Manufacturing principles in their business. The improvements lead to elimination of waste and improved efficiency, which in turn leads to lower costs. And what happens when those remodelers put a standard markup on less costs? Their price drops, right? So not only do they make less money, their position is compromised—especially if the lower prices brings them more in line with the Hyundais of their world.

As you can see, not having marketing involved in establishing the price of your services can undermine its ability to execute the positioning strategy. Certainly, marketing alone doesn't determine the price of your offerings (though some companies do operate this way), but marketing most certainly deserves a seat at the table.

There are three boxes to check when developing your pricing. It should:

1. Enable you to reach your revenue goals.
2. Maximize your profits.
3. Reflect your position relative to your competitors.

Don't get me wrong. It's okay to have a standard markup as a starting point. After all, this is the simplest way to ensure profitability. But that shouldn't be the end of the conversation. You need to drill deeper to arrive at the right price. Analyze your competitors' prices and make sure your pricing reflects the value you deliver relative to the competition.

SECTION THREE

FINDING THE LOBSTER LOVERS

I'm gonna make him an offer he can't refuse.

—Don Corleone, *The Godfather*

FIFTEEN
MESSAGING

NOW THAT YOU HAVE A POSITIONING STATEMENT, IT'S time to communicate your position to the world. But you can't just take your positioning statement and plaster it everywhere. Quite the opposite. Your positioning statement is an internal document that should never be shared.

What we need to do is translate your positioning statement into a strategic set of key points. Marketers call this strategic set *messaging*. Put simply, messaging is *what* your brand needs to talk about with your target audience.

The fastest way to undermine your positioning strategy is to have people who represent your brand communicate something that conflicts with your positioning statement. Messaging is the only way to be certain that everyone who represents your brand will do so in a way that aligns with your position. This ensures brand consistency.

Develop Your Messaging

The goal of messaging is to articulate what your Point of Difference and your Reasons to Believe mean *to your target of one*. Think in terms of your target's interests, desires, and beliefs.

For example, we've established that Fluffy Decks' Point of Difference is that they "*make family health and safety their top priority*." What does this mean to our stay-at-home mom? It means her family can "enjoy the outdoors injury-free." This is a messaging statement for the fourth stone. I say ***a*** messaging statement because it's okay to have multiple messages for each of the fourth and fifth Positioning Stones.

As you develop your messaging, keep in mind which messages address your target's functional needs, and which address the emotional needs. You may also want to consider using examples.

I find it easiest to work with a table when creating my messaging statements. A completed table for Fluffy Decks is illustrated below.

	Positioning	**Messaging**
POD	Makes family health and safety its top priority.	• Enjoy the outdoors injury free
RTB1	We have a zero percent exposed wood policy on every deck we build	• Splinters are a thing of the past • Health risks assoc. with prolonged contact with chemically treated lumber is avoided.
RTB2	All decks must pass the ADI 18-Point Family Safety Standards® test	• Our proprietary safety standards go far beyond the minimum code req's our competitors meet. (list examples)

Don't be too concerned with wordiness or eloquence. Messaging statements aren't supposed to be ad-ready phrases. They simply define what it is your brand needs to be talking about. So avoid catchy phrases and cute punchlines. Keep your statements simple, clear, and concise. They should be matter-of-fact.

Before finalizing, ensure that the messaging as a whole passes the CHAD test.

- Clarity—leave no room for ambiguity or individual interpretation.
- Heart—make sure that at least some of the message statements address the target's emotional needs.

- Alignment—verify that the messages directly convey the spirit of its respective Positioning Stone.
- Differentiation—in its entirety, your messaging must set you apart from your competition.

SIXTEEN
COPYWRITING

WHERE YOUR MESSAGING DEFINES WHAT YOUR BRAND must communicate, copy is *how* your brand says it. It's the content that both creates interest and turns it into action. In short, copywriting is writing to persuade.

Copy*writers*, therefore, are people who have studied this art. And believe me when I say that it *is* a studied art. Volumes have been written on the subject. If you are not a student of the craft, I recommend you outsource this critical job to someone who is. While it is true that good copywriters can be a bit pricey, they pay for themselves many times over in qualified leads and closed sales.

That being said, it may not be possible for you to have every marketing piece that goes out the door be drafted by a professional copywriter. So here is your crash course on DIY copywriting.

The Three Laws

I first read Isaac Asimov's *I, Robot* in the sixth grade. You may have seen the movie of the same name starring Will Smith. The movie bears no resemblance to the book, but it was inspired by it. More specifically, it was inspired by Asimov's elegant "Three Laws of Robotics," introduced in the second chapter. These laws were created to protect us from robots. They are:

1. A robot may not harm a human being, or, through inaction, allow a human being to come to harm.

2. A robot must obey the orders given to it by human beings, except where such orders would conflict with the first law.
3. A robot must protect its own existence, as long as such protection does not conflict the first or second law.

I absolutely adore the beauty of the cascading directives, which build on each other to ensure the safety of humankind. The moment I read them, I knew I wanted to be a science fiction writer. (I guess I was half-right.)

And so, with a tip of the hat to Asimov's brilliance, I created the *Three Laws of Copy* to protect your marketing from bad writing. A copywriter shall never violate these laws, *ever*:

1. A copywriter must speak with empathy to the wants, needs, and desires of the brand's target customer.
2. A copywriter must convey the brand's point of difference, except where such communication would conflict with the first law.
3. A copywriter must simplify and cut ruthlessly, as long as such action does not conflict with the first or second law.

If you learn nothing else from this chapter, learn the three laws. Even mediocre writers can compose effective copy if they obey them.

The Three Flaws

Seeing as how we're coming off the Three Laws, I was tempted to change this section to the three shortcomings, but that doesn't exactly roll off the tongue. No matter. I can't change the fact that there are three flaws in the human brain: The Castaway Bias, The Craving, and Lennon's Dream. To write compelling—virtually hypnotic—copy, you must leverage these psychological shortcomings in your target audience.

Flaw One: The Castaway Bias

Imagine for a moment you're shipwrecked on an island with a volleyball and no means of communication other than the time-honored message in a bottle. What would you write? It would probably be all about you, right?

Help *me*! *My* name is... *I'm* stranded on... *I* was traveling on a boat... *I'm* on an island... *My* destination was... *I* don't have any food...

Me, me, me.

What's more, you are writing without regard for who reads your message. You don't care if it's a man, woman, or child. Just so long as they can read, they qualify as your target audience.

Tsk, tsk.

And finally, what do you do with this message when you're done? You throw it into the sea, hoping whoever stumbles upon it will stop, open it, and read it.

This illustrates the most common mistake novices make when writing copy. They think like a castaway. They write all about themselves, their products, and their services. They write without regard for who is reading it, and then they cast it out into the world and hope it will be read.

(You may have noticed that this tendency is addressed by the first law of copy.)

Look, I'm not judging. It's not your fault. It's a quite literally a flaw in our wiring. We are, fundamentally, an egocentric species. We love talking about ourselves. We want to share our interests, desires, and goals with anyone who will listen. I'm sure you've encountered the proud parent who can't stop showing off family pictures. Or the health nut that has a new "fascinating" exercise story every time you run into them. Heck, satisfying this psychological need is pretty much the only reason Facebook exists.

This isn't conjecture. Study after study has shown that our favorite topic of conversation is, hands down, ourselves. Why? Because it's gratifying. Literally. One study revealed that when subjects talked about themselves, the areas of the brain that lit up were the same areas that light up when taking drugs and having sex. Simply put, *me, my*, and *I* feel *really* good to say.

To combat this hardwired flaw in the brain, the trained copywriter turns to one magical word: *you.*

You is arguably the most powerful word in the copywriter's arsenal, and there are three reasons why.

1. If you're using it, you can't fall victim to the Castaway Bias.
2. It helps you take advantage of the flaw in your target's mind, because you're talking about them. (Yes, we also like to have others talk about our needs and desires).
3. It ensures your copy speaks to *one* person. Strong copy is always a one-on-one conversation. It's rarely a good idea to address the masses when writing to persuade.

This third reason is of particular importance. Copywriting novices love to talk to *everyone.* Here are a few real-world examples from websites I've audited in which the writer addressed the masses. Note the impact of changing it to a one-on-one conversation.

Weak copy: We believe everyone deserves to live in style.

Stronger version: You deserve to live in style.

Weak copy: We take great pride in working closely with our clients.

Stronger version: We'll work closely with you.

Weak copy: Business owners can double their profits.

Stronger version: Double your profits.

You can see it doesn't take much to improve weak copy. But if you want to write the strongest possible copy, you need to do more than swap pronouns.

I have a tool I use when writing copy that has never failed me. I hope it gives you the same level of success. I call it the *Lucy Letter*. Early on in my career I struggled, like most, to write one-on-one copy. I realize now that my struggles were rooted in fear—fear of writing something that didn't make sense to the person reading it. After all, how could I possibly write something personal that makes sense to everyone?

Obviously, the problem was that I was *trying* to write to everyone. Copy should always be written with your target in mind. But even after overcoming that mistake, I continued to struggle. My copy fell flat. Then, one day, it happened. I discovered this powerful copywriting tool, and I found it quite by accident.

I was marketing director for a remodeling company, and we wanted to add a handyman division. We decided to do a soft launch and roll it out quietly to test the waters and gauge interest. The plan was to reach out to our best past clients individually, tell them about the new service, and see if they would sign up.

The first email I composed was to Lucy. Lucy was by far the best customer we had ever had. She was the personification of our target customer. If I could have cloned one person on earth to purchase our services, it would have been Lucy. So it was a no-brainer to reach out to her first.

After composing the email and checking for typos and grammatical errors, I read through it one last time, as I always do before hitting the send button (you can never be too cautious). And that's when it happened. The ah-ha moment. I didn't need to write to my target *market*, I needed to write to one person *within* that target. I needed to write to Lucy.

That email written specifically for Lucy ended up going out to everyone. And it performed beautifully.

In the years since, I've used the Lucy Letter concept with many clients with great success. So if you're struggling to write powerful one-on-one copy that converts, go into your customer database, and dig out the greatest customer you've ever had—the one that is the embodiment of your target market. Go find *your* Lucy, and write her a letter.

Flaw Two: The Craving

The second flaw of the brain is its incessant need for answers. It's virtually impossible to *willingly* accept something without an explanation as to why it is so. We need to know the reasons why. We crave it.

We have been asking the question since we learned to talk. Why is the sky blue? Why does the wind blow? Why don't things fall up? Where does lightning come from?

It's like an itch you can't reach. And that need to scratch it stays with us our entire life.

But just as with the Castaway Bias, there's one magic word that copywriters use to ensure they scratch that itch. That word is *because*. Plug that word into anything you are writing, and you've successfully painted yourself into a corner. The only way out is to scratch the reader's itch.

Now, with a child you can get away with pretty much anything to scratch the itch and send them on their way. Like, "Oh, that's just the angels bowling" (this was my mother-in-law's answer to "Where does lightning come from?" when my son asked her).

But that doesn't cut it with an adult. We grown-ups need reasons, and they had better be legitimate. Right?

Well, kind of.

Because is so effective at scratching the itch, it's mesmerizing. Copywriters have known about its hypnotic strength since the early 1900s, but a psychological study conducted in the late 1970s confirmed it.

I first heard about Dr. Ellen Langer's study when reading Robert Cialdini's 1984 book, *Influence: The Psychology of Persuasion.* (As a side note, this is an excellent book. I consider it requisite reading for anyone who wants to be a successful marketer.)

Dr. Langer's study, which was published in the *Journal of Personality and Social Psychology* in 1978, beautifully illustrates the power of *because.*

For the experiment, researchers went to the City University of New York graduate center and approached people waiting in line to make copies. Their goal was to see if they could get people to let them cut ahead in the line.

To establish the baseline, researchers asked the control group, "Excuse me, I have five pages. May I use the Xerox machine?" As you can see, the researcher provides no reason for the request. This got 60 percent of the subjects to agree.

For the treatment group, researchers added a reason—a *because.* The question was appended to, "Excuse me, I have five pages. May I use the Xerox machine because I'm in a rush?" The small change made a big difference. This time, researchers got 94 percent of the subjects to agree to their request. Clearly, adding the *because* made a significant impact on their ability to influence the people waiting in line.

However, researchers weren't finished. Since the reason given to the treatment group was a legitimate one (I'm in a rush), this only proved that subjects were persuaded by the argument.

If this were a drug study, the persuasiveness of the argument would be considered the active ingredient in the medication they were testing.

So the researchers needed to run the test with a placebo group, one that gave subjects a sugar pill. In other words, no persuasive arguments.

What they came up with was, "Excuse me, I have five pages. May I use the Xerox machine *because I have to make copies*?" This variation with a nonsensical reason (obviously, you have to make copies—you're asking to use the copier) was called *placebic information* by the researchers.

The results were fascinating. Where the legitimate reason of being in a rush got 94 percent of the subjects to agree, the nonsensical reason got 93 percent to agree! It was clear that the mere act of giving a reason (saying *because*) was all that was needed to persuade people.

The point here, however, isn't to suggest that you can write any bit of nonsense after saying because and you will influence others. There's a proportional relationship between the strength of the *because* and what is at stake. You can't, for example, say to a prospect, "You should buy this car because you need to drive places" and think they're going to write you a check.

Dr. Langer's study proved this concept of proportionality as well. When researchers increased the number of pages from five to twenty, the nonsensical reason didn't yield any advantage. (However, the legitimate reason was still much more effective, nearly doubling the result of the control group.)

There you have it. Clinical proof. I've just given you the *because* for why you need to use *because*. (That's so meta.)

Flaw Three: Lennon's Dream

The third flaw is a fantastical journey into the human brain. It's a story that, on its face, will seem more science fiction than science fact.

In 1971, John Lennon released "Imagine," a song that inspires you to imagine a better world. A world without borders or religion or material possessions, and therefore, no greed or hunger or vengeance. A world at peace. Sounds good to me.

While he may not have known it at the time, Lennon's dream of a better world displayed an undeniable flaw in the human brain: it cannot tell the difference between imagination and reality.

It seems absurd, I know. But it's true. The physiological processes in the brain are the same whether you experience something or just imagine it.

Before I continue, a quick aside: as I write this, I'm sitting at the bar of a nearby Chili's restaurant. (I thought a change of scenery would be good for my writing. Plus, it's lunchtime, and I'm hungry. So, two birds.)

Anyway, I'm looking through the menu, *trying* to be good. I could stand to lose a pound or two. But, like I said, I am pretty hungry. So despite my best efforts, I can't help but look at the handcrafted burgers section of the menu.

The *Alex's Santa Fe Burger* caught my eye. The description reads, "Yes, Chef Alex is real. And so are his burger skills. Stacked high with avocado, pepper jack, red onion, roasted jalapeños, tomato, pickles, cilantro, and spicy Santa Fe sauce."

Man, that sounds good.

And the picture isn't helping my resolve. The burger is sitting on a wooden board with a steak knife driven into its center. The wet slather of spicy Santa Fe sauce is dripping down the sides of a thick, glistening, perfectly cooked patty. I can just imagine the glorious mess of the first bite as the juice from the patty runs down my thumbs and the melted pepper jack cheese stretches when I pull the burger from my mouth.

Yeah, I don't think the salad is happening today.

Moving on, did you know that we need saliva to eat? It helps the teeth chew, and it prepares the food for digestion. Our brain increases the secretion of saliva when we eat. I mention it because, since the brain (in and of itself) can't discern the difference between something that I'm thinking about doing and something that's actually happening, it starts secreting saliva. My mouth is literally watering right now—watering something fierce.

It's funny. I'm writing about the power of the word *imagine,* and my mouth starts watering from reading a menu. The irony of this moment could not go unmentioned.

If you think about it, this phenomenon shouldn't be surprising in the least. After all, what *is* the difference between imagination and reality? There's only one thing: the origin of the stimuli. That's it.

Consider this. If I say, "Think of a kangaroo," you're now thinking of a kangaroo. There's no way you don't see it in your mind's eye. So, what's happened? Well, in layman's terms, your brain went into the card catalog of your mind, found the kangaroo card, and said, "Here it is. This is a kangaroo."

Now, in contrast, what would happen if you were to look over your left shoulder and *see* a kangaroo? The exact same thing! The only difference is your brain got the message from your eyes this time, instead of from me. After that, it was business as usual. Your brain went into the card catalog of your mind, found the kangaroo card, and said, "Here it is. That's a kangaroo."

Copywriters have known about this backdoor into the unconscious mind for some time. By using *imagine*, you can get your prospects to genuinely experience anything you want. It is a magical ability indeed.

Imagine in Action

My editor wanted me to remove this example because our 45th president is deeply divisive. But this has nothing to do with politics or agenda. It's simply a real life example of the power of *imagine*. Please don't read anything into it or make it more than what it is: a marketing case study. In here, we're all just marketers.

It was 2015. The Republican presidential primary election was in full swing, and Republican candidate Donald Trump was leading in all the polls. Many pundits were calling him the favorite to clinch the Republican nomination.

As Trump's odds of winning the nomination grew, I began hearing the same phrase. "I can't imagine Trump as president." I heard it at the office. I overhead people at the gym. I even heard it outside of church.

I'm not exaggerating for effect when I say I heard it everywhere. Heck, even guys at a barber shop I stopped in during a business trip were saying it, and let's just say that this was a place in which John Wayne was represented by way of four posters and a life-size cardboard standup.

Being the marketer that I am, I was curious to see what Trump's strategists were going to do to temper this sentiment. After all, if I was hearing it everywhere, then so was Trump's team.

I didn't have to wait long to get the answer. In mid-September, I turned on the news to see Donald Trump looking, well, presidential. He stood on the deck of the USS *Iowa* addressing crowds of supporters. Behind him was a battery of sixteen-inch cannons that had seen a lot of action in World War II. On the deck, posted at the corners of the small stage, stood four secret service agents in their black suits and dark sunglasses. It was brilliant (from a marketing perspective). Now people *could* imagine Trump as president because they'd already seen him looking like one. I'm not saying this one appearance was the sole reason he won the election, but it certainly helped.

As this example demonstrates, you don't have to literally say the word *imagine* to take advantage of its awesome power. Similarly, some remodeling contractors I know let prospective clients "walk through" their new kitchen before they even sign a contract by using virtual reality glasses and 3-D modeling.

Regardless of whether you help people imagine through demonstration, or you use the word in your copy, as I did with the cheeseburger (which just arrived, by the way), one thing is certain. Getting your target to imagine themselves in your copy is just as good as getting them to experience it firsthand.

The Copywriter's Secret Weapon

As I mentioned, good copywriters can command a pretty penny. In fact, some of the highest-paid writers on the planet aren't novelists, they're copywriters. It can be expensive to hire these pros on a freelance basis and, for most, having them on staff is flat-out crazy. But samples of their work—the techniques and strategies they use—are all around you.

Every day, you are bombarded with advertising messages. Even the most conservative estimates say you're exposed to 5,000 of them per day. Many are the result of countless hours of work by skilled copywriters: samples of great calls to action, persuasive headlines, layouts, and more. And they're sending them to you for free.

Don't discard this treasure trove of work. Keep it. Create a swipe file.

Despite the shady name, swipe files are not illegal nor unethical. Every copywriter worth his salt has a swipe file. In fact, if you were to take a copywriting course, you would most likely be required to start building your own as part of the curriculum.

Your swipe file is where you keep any piece of marketing communication that stands out to you. This includes sales letters, print ads, postcards, emails, banner ads, and so on.

Did you notice I included emails in that list? I have to say, unless the content is pure garbage, you should never unsubscribe from an email list. They are often a goldmine of good copy. I'm subscribed to well over 100 different email lists. Naturally, many of them go unread. But the ones I do open are invaluable.

Why? Because I opened them!

Something about *that* subject line worked on me, so I'll move that email to my subject-line swipe folder. And yes, you should break your swipe file down into subfolders. I recommend filing by anatomy, like headlines, calls to action, layouts, and so forth, because it's easier to locate the inspiration I need when I'm stuck.

Did you notice I said *inspiration*? It's important to understand that your swipe file is meant to inspire, not to be plagiarized. For one thing, straight out duplication isn't likely to work. The copy you're looking at was crafted for a different target (namely, you) with different messaging in mind. So use it as a catalyst only. It's a fantastic resource when you know what you want to say, but you're not quite sure how to say it. That's when a little inspiration will go a long way.

Equipped with your swipe file, you'll be able to tackle any campaign, from client letters to print ads. It's like having your very own copywriting consultant on call twenty-four hours a day.

Tradecraft

Everything in this chapter, from obeying the *Three Laws of Copy* to leveraging the *Three Flaws of the Human Brain* are critical concepts used by elite copywriters. When used in conjunction with the following tips, you will be able craft some serious, lead-converting copy.

- Write short, simple sentences.
- Write the way you talk.
- Begin sentences with conjunctions. But, and, or, for. It's not grammatically correct, but that's okay.
- Use one or two sentence paragraphs at most.

- Make it skimmable. Use graphical writing techniques to make words and phrases stand out, such as:
    - Subheads and crossheads to break up the copy.
    - Underlines, italics, highlighting, call outs.
    - Bulleted lists.
- Tell a story.

Don't forget: it takes more than knowing a few tips and techniques to consistently pump out winning copy. Like any other skill, it takes study and practice. Have patience and commit to the craft. Proficiency doesn't happen overnight.

If you really want to get serious about honing your skills, I recommend reading books dedicated to the craft, or better yet, joining a community of copywriting professionals who work together for continual improvement. These communities have training centers, workshops, webinars, and more. For a list of recommended resources, visit BeTheLobster.com/outside-resources.

SEVENTEEN
PUTTING IT ALL TOGETHER

LET'S CLOSE OUT THIS SECTION ON MESSAGING AND copywriting with an exercise. Put what you've learned into action by creating a promotional email or an advertisement for our fictional deck builder, Fluffy Decks, LLC.

As a reminder, our positioning statement is:

> For THE STAY-AT-HOME MOM IN HER THIRTIES WITH YOUNG CHILDREN who WANTS PEACE OF MIND that HER KIDS WILL ALWAYS BE SAFE, FLUFFY DECKS IS THE PREMIER FAMILY-OWNED DECK BUILDER THAT MAKES FAMILY HEALTH AND SAFETY ITS TOP PRIORITY because WE HAVE A "NO-EXPOSED-WOOD" POLICY ON EVERY DECK WE BUILD AND all DECKS MUST PASS THE ADI EIGHTEEN-POINT FAMILY SAFETY STANDARDS TEST. We convey this by being A SINCERE, KIND, THOUGHTFUL, NURTURING, AND CARING COMPANY WITH A STRONG BELIEF IN FAMILY VALUES.

Our three messaging statements that were derived from this positioning statement are below:

- Point of Difference: Enjoy the outdoors injury-free.
- Reason to Believe One: Splinters are a thing of the past, and health risks associated with prolonged contact with chemically treated lumber are avoided.

- Reason to Believe Two: Our proprietary safety standards go far beyond the minimum government requirements that our competitors must meet.

I've created a sample ad for comparison.

EXERCISE:

Take a minute to break it down. Consider:

- Does it stay true to our positioning statement?
- Is it speaking to our target market? Is the unmet need being addressed?
- Is it in line with the messages we've identified in our messaging table? Which ones?
- Does the ad convey our brand personality?
- Does it obey the three laws?

Which copywriting secrets from this chapter were used?

Now, apply the same questions and critical eye to your ad copy.

Your
child's safety is
our top priority.
That's why *every* deck
we build is vinyl wrapped
and 100% splinter-free.
(Yes, it costs us more.)
But if it means tiny toes
can enjoy the open-air
boo-boo free, then we
are happy to do it.
Because an out-
door tea party
with mommy?
Well, that's the
bestest day ever.

Decks (and tea parties) in a Day

CALL FLUFFY DECKS NOW
FOR A FREE ESTIMATE

SECTION FOUR

EVEN LOBSTERS NEED A PLAN

If you're reading this, you can read.

—Captain Obvious

EIGHTEEN
CREATING A STRATEGIC MARKETING PLAN

HAVING A PLAN IS CRITICAL TO SUCCESS. EVERYONE knows that. It's like something Captain Obvious would say. Why then, do you suppose, do business owners and marketers alike consistently skip the planning phase and jump straight to executing tactics?

Don't get me wrong, not everyone is guilty. Some do make the effort.

I'm often sent marketing plans for review from friends and colleagues. It's not an intensive formal review, mind you. It's more like a, "Mark, could you take a look and let me know if you see any red flags?" kind of thing.

Unfortunately, I almost always see a red flag. What's worse, it's usually the same flag. I just counted, and of the last seven marketing plans I received, six of them suffered from it: none of them were marketing plans.

That's right. What was sent under the guise of a marketing plan was, in actuality, nothing more than a marketing *budget*, a list of tactics with dollar amounts assigned. Don't feel bad if you, too, have a budget that plays the role of a marketing plan. Upward of 90 percent of small-to-medium-sized businesses work off budgets instead of strategic plans.

This is, however, a colossal mistake.

Before we dive into it, a clarification is in order. The definition of *marketing plan* is somewhat up in the air. If you Google it, you'll find (literally) billions of results, and not all of them agree with one another. Some define a marketing plan as a comprehensive document that outlines *everything* involved in marketing for the company, from positioning to messaging, from pricing strategy to SWOT analysis. Nothing is left out of a marketing plan. It's essentially your company's marketing manifesto, and is usually one component of the company business plan.

The thing is, this type of marketing plan has many elements that could remain unchanged for years, such as identifying the target market, outlining pricing strategy, and defining messaging. So for the purposes of this book, I'm defining it as a strategic plan that is updated annually. Its purpose is to outline how the company is going to achieve its goals for the coming year.

This section is dedicated to developing this plan, which consists of six *linear* elements:

1. Objectives
2. Strategies
3. Tactics
4. Budget
5. Metrics
6. Decision

Linear is the key word in that statement. You *must* work through them in this order. It's like baseball. You can't go to second until you've reached first. Speaking of which, you may have noticed that *budget* is step four of this run around the bases. (Just saying).

Step One: Define the Objectives

Objectives are the goals of your marketing efforts. They must be specific and measurable. In addition, your objectives must be tied to a specific time frame. An objective without a deadline is a wish.

For example, your objective could be to increase qualified leads from ten per month to twenty per month by the end of December.

Step Two: Identify the Strategy

Strategy is often confused with tactics, and for that reason, this step trips most people up. In the most basic terms, strategy is the *how*, and tactics are the *what*. Strategy is a concept. It's how you will achieve your objective.

There's one simple test to determine if you've stated a strategy or a tactic. Ask yourself if it's something you can do or something you can buy. If the answer to both is no, then congratulations, you've successfully identified a strategy. If the answer to either is yes, then you've identified a tactic.

It may be easier to understand by way of example, so let us apply the do-or-buy test to weight loss. We'll ask the question, "Can you lose weight?"

Take your time and think carefully. Do you have the answer?

Are you sure?

The answer is no, you can't buy or do that. To actually lose weight would mean you would have to be walking down the street and suddenly realize twelve pounds went missing. Can you imagine? You would look down and start patting your waist as if you had misplaced your keys and wonder, *What did I do with that twelve pounds?*

If you're still doubting me, I challenge you to describe the activity of losing weight. Odds are you have a list of *other* activities coming to mind. That's because losing weight is a strategy, and you can't do strategies.

Let's work this weight loss example from the top to so you can see it in action.

First, you define the objective. Let's say your objective is to look good for your sister's wedding in the spring (not exactly specific and measurable, but good enough for an example).

How can you achieve that goal? (Strategy is the *how*). Well, one way would be to look younger. Another way would be to lose weight. Let's choose the strategy *lose weight*.

Next, you determine the tactics. List *what* you need to do to execute the strategy. You can eat broccoli, avoid cake, run daily, take the stairs instead of elevators, count calories, fast, sit in a steam room, and so on.

See how that works?

Let's go back for a moment. What if we had chosen the other strategy, *look younger*? What tactics could you utilize to execute *that* strategy? Some tactics include using skincare products, getting an acid peel, growing long bangs, using concealer, exercising, and getting a facelift.

As you can see, the strategy you select directly influences the tactics you must use.

Here's an exercise to help you practice finding strategies using a real-world marketing example. Earlier, I gave a sample objective to increase qualified leads from ten per month to twenty per month by the end of December.

What are strategies you could use to achieve that goal? There are quite a few of them. What can you come up with? Here are two to get you started.

1. Get more referrals. If I can get more past clients to refer more people, I will increase my qualified leads.
2. Raise brand awareness. If more people know my company exists, then it stands to reason that my incoming leads would increase.
3. ____________________
4. ____________________
5. ____________________

Something to bear in mind when working on your strategic plan: at this point in the process, you're not making final decisions. You are brainstorming. There's nothing wrong with having five or more strategies identified that will meet your objective. You will pare it down in step six.

Step Three: Lay Out the Tactics

Now that you know what strategies you could use to achieve your goal, you may begin identifying the specific tactics to execute them.

To illustrate this by way of example, let's continue the exercise.

Strategy One: Get More Referrals

Some tactics to execute this strategy would include the following:

- Send out holiday cards (to stay top of mind).
- Start a weekly e-newsletter (to stay top of mind).
- Create a referral reward program.
- Call past clients and start asking for referrals.
- ______________________________
- ______________________________

Strategy Two: Raise Brand Awareness

Some tactics to execute this strategy would include the following:

- Billboard advertising.
- Run magazine advertisements.
- Increase social media presence.
- Wrap company vehicles with bumper-to-bumper branding.
- ______________________________
- ______________________________

As you can see once again, the tactics you use change dramatically based on the strategy you choose to deploy.

Use a planning table like the one below to organize your thoughts. You can download a free copy by visiting BeTheLobster.com/planning-table.

PLANNING TABLE

OBJECTIVE	STRATEGIES	TACTICS	EST.COST	SUBTOTAL	METRICS
Primary Objective	Strategy 1	1.			
		2.			
		3.			
	Strategy 2	1.			
		2.			
		3.			
		4.			
		5.			
	Strategy 3	1.			
		2.			
		3.			
			TOTAL:	$	

Step Four: Budget

Now, we're (finally) ready to move onto budgeting. Using the Budget columns of our planning table, insert the estimated amount it will cost to execute the individual tactics per unit. Depending on the tactic, the units could be time-based (per week, per month, per year, etc.) or quantity-based (per lead, per each, per attendee, etc.). Enter the estimated annual expenditure for each tactic in the subtotal column, and total the entire column at the bottom.

Step Five: Metrics

Next, identify the metrics you will use to measure success. For each tactic, identify the metric and fill in the metrics column of your table. Common metrics include CTR (click-through rate), CAC (customer acquisition cost), number of attendees, number of retweets/likes/shares, and so on.

This is important because the degree to which you're able to measure success could be a determining factor as to whether or not you move forward with a particular tactic.

Note: If you will have more than one marketing objective for the year, return to step one now and complete a planning table for each additional objective prior to moving on to step six.

Step Six: Decision Time

The resulting planning table(s) represent your optimal plan for accomplishing each of the respective marketing objectives you've identified. There is a very good chance, however, that the total expense to execute these plans is more than your marketing budget will allow. So you must whittle them down to a state that fits within your budget without compromising the plan's effectiveness.

Generally speaking, it's better to forgo an entire strategy than it is to keep all of them and cut out a few tactics in each. If, for example, you have four strategies for the stated objective, and you're overbudget, consider removing an entire strategy (and, therefore, all the tactics within it). If you're still overbudget, then begin dropping individual tactics. Again, this is more of a guideline than a rule.

But how do you decide which strategies and tactics should stay and which must go? Well, whatever you do, don't make your decisions based solely on cost. Your decision should be made taking several factors into account, including time investment, effectiveness, risk versus reward, and so on.

To assist in your decision-making process, I've included a definitive list of marketing tactics in Appendix B. Each tactic is rated on five factors: Time to Launch, Time to Outcome, Potency, Cost, and Skill Level. Use it as a guide—but don't disregard good old-fashioned intuition. While it may be tempting to think that every decision should be made by systematically weighing all factors, gut instinct is a powerful force that has served humankind well. Strategic planning is as much art as science. At the end of the day, this is an exercise in prophecy, so don't ignore your gut.

SECTION FIVE

EXECUTION (OF TACTICS, NOT LOBSTERS)

Here's where the fun begins.

—Han Solo, *Star Wars*

NINETEEN
THE WONDERFUL WORLD OF TACTICS

FOR MOST, THIS IS THE FUN PART OF THE JOB: THE execution of tactics. Sending a message out into the world and seeing qualified leads come pouring in is one of the purest joys of business. I'm a bit unique in that I like the failures almost as much as the successes. There is so much knowledge gained in them. And trying to discover why one variation works beautifully while another fails miserably? Fascinating.

Romanticized ballads of marketing aside, tactics are the nuts and bolts of it all. And knowing how to execute them effectively is critical. As I mentioned in the previous chapter, I've included a list of marketing tactics in Appendix B. Each tactic is rated on five factors: Time to Launch, Time to Outcome, Potency, Cost, and Skill Level. The scores are based on my experience and typical business scenarios. However, the score could differ for you. For example, the Time to Launch score for a website is five out of five (long-time). But if you have a web developer on staff, then you may want to drop that score to a three. For that reason, I've created an Excel-based spreadsheet so you may change scores and weight factors to suit your circumstances. You can download it by visiting BeTheLobster.com/tactics-spreadsheet.

But remember: this is just another tool to assist you in your decision-making process. Don't blindly select tactics based on the final ranking of tactics on the spreadsheet.

In the remaining chapters of this section, we'll dive deeper into a handful of tactics that virtually every business utilizes. And I'll also share some opportunities that I guarantee you are missing out on.

TWENTY
REFERRALS AND WORD OF MOUTH

ARGUABLY, THE MOST RELIED-UPON LEAD-GENERATING tactic by small and medium businesses is customer referrals. So to not dedicate a chapter to its execution would be marketing book malpractice.

Referrals are the proverbial Holy Grail of sales leads. And it's no wonder why. Referral clients come to you on the word of people they trust, be they family, friend, or colleague. This effectively transfers some of that trust onto you. How much trust is transferred depends on two things: the nature of their relationship with each other, and the extent to which you were talked up.

Consider the difference between "I know a roofing guy you can call" and "If you don't call Johnny, you're a fool. I will personally guarantee he fixes your problem." Clearly, some referred leads are going to be stronger than others. But what can you do about it? Believe it or not, you have more control than you think. And it's through formal referral and word-of-mouth marketing campaigns.

Oftentimes, the terms *referral* and *word of mouth* are used interchangeably; however, while they are similar, there is a distinct difference between the two. In the simplest terms, if you give someone something in exchange for a lead or a sale, it's referral marketing. If you do not give an incentive, it's word-of-mouth marketing. Both are effective marketing strategies, and neither should be left to chance, so understanding the distinction will help you create programs that will influence them both.

Referral Marketing

Referral marketing requires incentives and reward to get your customers to participate. Reward can come in many forms, including discounts, cash back, free products, early access, free upgrades, company merchandise, VIP status, and more.

To some, it seems crass to pay for referrals, but there are significant benefits to this *quid pro quo* arrangement. For one thing, you are essentially employing your entire list of current and past customers to *actively* promote your company to their networks. And having hundreds or even thousands of people actively working on your behalf is a wonderful thing. In fact, if the reward is valuable enough, some will invest significant time and effort into the endeavor. This is a powerful asset to help expand your base.

Another benefit is that it encourages your promoters to spend more money with you, especially if the reward is a discount on your products and services—which brings me to a couple of dos and don'ts of a good referral program. *Don't* reward your promoters with something that has nothing to do with your brand. Yes, you may get more referrals by offering a free iPad than by offering a free appetizer, but the disconnect undermines the value you deliver. Payment or not, you still want your promoters to be thinking about how great *your* brand is, not how great someone else's brand is. Besides, a free appetizer means they'll have to come in and buy dinner, too.

Do be sure the incentives align with the purpose of your business. A referral marketing program should serve to not only bring in new referrals, but also to increase your existing customer's connection with you.

Word-of-Mouth Marketing

Some say that relying on word of mouth is a waste of time because all you do is sit back and hope. Well, if all you're doing is waiting for people to recommend you on their own, then you would be right; that *is* a colossal waste of time. But waiting and hoping is not *doing* word-of-mouth marketing. In fact, that's not doing *anything*.

While it is true that word of mouth happens organically, it is still something you can (and should) influence. It takes a concerted effort on your part to encourage your customers to tell your story.

A successful word-of-mouth campaign requires two things: a story worth telling and an audience willing to hear it. Your customers provide the audience willing to hear it, so you have to provide the story worth telling. But what are stories worth telling? In short, things that are remarkable.

There's a term in psychology I want you to become intimately familiar with: *schema*. Hang it on your refrigerator. Stick it on your desk. Glue it to your dashboard. Because it's going to change the way you look at word of mouth forever, and I don't want you to forget it.

Schemas are sets of preconceived ideas that your brain has formed based on past life experiences. Put simply, a schema is something we know to be true. For example, if you go to a restaurant, pull out the chair, and sit, what will happen? Nothing of consequence, right? You'll just be sitting on a chair at the dinner table.

The fact that the chair will support you is a schema. It's a shortcut that your brain has developed on how it thinks the world *should* work. If you didn't have that schema, you wouldn't sit in a chair without first inspecting it thoroughly, pushing down on the seat, wiggling the legs, and examining the back.

But you don't do that. You already know the chair will support you. It's a foregone conclusion.

What does this have to do with word-of-mouth marketing? Well, as I said, word of mouth requires a story worth telling, and the stories we tell *break* schemas.

Imagine for a moment you're in that same restaurant, and you see someone take a seat at the table across from you, only to have the chair collapse beneath him the moment his bottom touches the seat. The legs explode outward as he drops. He desperately reaches for the table in a futile attempt to save himself before coming to rest on a pile of debris.

Do you think that's a story you might tell others about? Of course it is. In fact, I'd bet dollars to donuts that most people would be posting pictures to Facebook before the last leg landed. Such is the power of breaking a schema.

So how does this apply to business? Let's look at one example you may have experienced firsthand. You're seated at a booth in a restaurant. The waiter comes up to the table and says, "How ya'll doin'?" and sits down as if he's going to join you for dinner, forcing you to slide over to make room. He takes your order like a student taking notes at his desk, and then stands and leaves.

For most, this is not the normal behavior we have come to expect from our servers. And if you've had this happen to you, then you probably had a brief discussion about the experience with others at your table as soon as he left with your order. Whether or not you went on to tell the story to others in the days that followed would depend on how deeply rooted this particular schema is for *you*.

This is at the core of how far the word of mouth will travel. How deeply rooted is the schema to the person experiencing it?

Consider this. If I threw a brick at a window, and it bounced off, that would be odd, but not necessarily schema-breaking. There could be a number of reasons for that to happen, like that the window is made of Plexiglas. If, however, I throw a brick, and it floats away like a balloon—*that* will probably end up as the lead story on the evening news. Bricks breaking windows isn't as deeply rooted as bricks not floating in air.

Another key factor is the personal nature of schemas. Remember: schemas are shortcuts *your* brain makes on how it thinks the world should work. Not everyone shares all schemas.

Take our overly-friendly waiter. Consider how the experience would be viewed by a socialite, as opposed to a high school freshman.

This brings me to the most vital point to be made: the word-of-mouth door swings both ways. Before breaking a schema, be certain that it's something that will encourage positive storytelling. I've had people tell me about "the waiter who sat at our table," and it's not always told in a positive light. *Uncomfortable, awkward, weird*, and *unprofessional* are just some of the adjectives used to tell the story—certainly not what the restaurant was going for with this strategy. So use caution, think it through, and consider your target audience. The best word-of-mouth strategy will break a schema your entire audience shares *and* will break it in a positive light.

EXERCISE:

Brainstorm schemas in your industry. What are things people know to be true when working with companies like yours? How do the employees behave? What does a typical transaction look like? Map out the entire experience. Write down even the most mundane components because, quite frankly, those are where the schemas lie. Then try to find ways that your business can break the schema in a positive way.

TWENTY-ONE
BLOGGING FOR SALES LEADS

BLOGGING IS THE FOUNDATION OF VIRTUALLY ANY effective SEO (search engine optimization) program. It's practically required if you want to have any chance of ranking in the top three spots of Google. But SEO is not the only reason to have a blog. It can also be a powerful lead generator for your company. It's so powerful that you can, in effect, plant and grow your very own customers.

Here's how:

Step One: Plant the Seeds

Planting a field of future customers comes down to five simple yet powerful words: you must publish stories regularly.

Let's break down the two key points of this short statement:

1. **Regularly**. You must create a schedule and stick to it. Subscribers must know when your next issue is coming. They should come to anticipate it. Imagine if your local paper was delivered on Tuesday and Wednesday, and then you didn't see it for three weeks, and then it came on a Friday night. Then the Sunday after next. Sounds ludicrous, does it not?
2. **Stories**. Notice I didn't say posts, articles, or blogs. I said stories. When I say you should be blogging, I'm not talking about keyword-rich posts that will propel you to the top of search engine results, as your SEO company might say. I'm talking about creating dynamic, compelling, and entertaining stories *for humans*.

Don't get me wrong; SEO is important. And a top position on Google is a fantastic place to be. But you should consider top rankings a glorious and inevitable byproduct of blogging—not its sole purpose.

Besides, Google has gotten really smart. Gone are the days of writing for Google bots. The Google search engine algorithm is now named RankBrain, an AI learning machine. It no longer looks solely for keyword matches. It actually *understands* what a searcher is asking for. It turns searches into concepts and looks for pages that cover those concepts—whether or not the exact phrase exists on the page. The point is, it's identifying the intent behind what is written. It's learning to read like a human. So write like a human—*for humans*—and you will be rewarded.

The biggest challenge you may face when trying to regularly publish stories is consistently coming up with things to write about. This becomes exponentially easier if you take the time to develop a plan for your blog. Remember what Captain Obvious said in Chapter Eighteen: "Having a plan is critical to success." Determine your goal and that will, in turn, determine the type of content you should be creating.

For example, if the goal of your blog is to attract people who are looking to buy immediately, your content should be almost exclusively dedicated to answering questions active buyers need answered (e.g., *Ten Questions to Ask Before Hiring a Lawyer*). Alternately, if your goal is to nurture relationships and build a list, then you may want it to be a *how-to* blog, a resource that future clients will turn to for help (e.g., *How to Write a Cease-and-Desist Letter with Free Template*).

But still, sometimes writer's block strikes. So if you need a little extra inspiration, I created an Excel-based blog idea generator to help get those creative juices flowing. You can download it by visiting BeTheLobster.com/idea-generator.

Step Two: Water the Fields

You've planted the seeds, now you need to continuously water them. Your amazing stories are nothing more than words on a page if no one reads them. And blogging is not an "if you build it, they will come" venture. You need to put energy and resources into getting people to subscribe to your blog. Your BHAG (a *big hairy audacious goal*, as defined in the book, *Built to Last*) should be that every single person in your target market subscribes to and reads your blog. Pretty audacious, I know. But a little audacity is good.

Here are some keys to making that happen:

- Name your blog something other than *blog*.
- Have a blog subscription form on every page of your website.
- Share every story you post on social media.
- Ask your readers to share your posts.
- Boost the posts on social media to extend your reach (it's a pay-to-play world, after all).

Make sure your external communication asks people to subscribe to your blog: email signatures, invoices, estimates, proposals, brochures, catalogs, menus, everything.

Step Three: Talk to Them

You've heard it before. Talking to plants helps them grow. This could not be truer for growing your readers into customers.

Ask them questions. Ask for feedback on your stories. Start discussions in the comments section. This is the most important step in building the relationship with your readership. With every ask for feedback, you build trust. With every comment, you build a community.

As we established when we discussed referral marketing in the previous chapter, trust is ultimately what this great game of business is all about. And blogging is a fantastic vehicle for building trust at scale.

TWENTY-TWO
EMAIL MARKETING

I LOVE EMAIL MARKETING. IT'S ONE OF THE MOST effective marketing channels available and costs next to nothing to deploy. In fact, clocking in at a jaw-dropping 4,400 percent ROI (return on investment), you would be hard-pressed to find a better place to spend your marketing dollar.

Of course, to realize that level of return, you need to do a lot more than just send out an email now and then. It takes planning, commitment, and clear understanding of the many components of a successful email marketing program.

First, it's important to understand that, technically speaking, *any* email sent to a potential or current customer could be considered email marketing; however, most who say "email marketing" will be referring to the mass delivery of email to a list of subscribers by way of an email automation platform. It is in this context that this chapter has been written. Within its pages, you'll learn about the types of campaigns you can use, the types of emails you can send, and the steps you need to take to ensure your email gets read.

Campaign Types

Aside from the one-off e-blast that is sent out on an as-needed basis (not ideal), there are two types of email marketing campaigns at your disposal. Painfully, they have come to be referred to as *drip campaigns* and *nurture campaigns*. I despise this. Not *drip campaigns*—I don't have an issue with that one. Drips are time-based emails that "drip" out to your list at the intervals you've set. For example, a possible drip campaign sequence could look something like this:

- Day Zero: Email with free guide that was requested
- Day One: Overview of benefits
- Day Three: Invitation to a private webinar
- Day Seven: Invitation to a personal demo

See? Time-based emails dripping out over time—days one, three, and seven in this case. It makes perfect sense to call it a drip campaign.

Unfortunately, somewhere along the way, some guy in some office somewhere decided to call behavioral-based emails *nurture campaigns*. And because of that guy, I've wasted countless hours explaining and re-explaining the difference.

Consider the definition of *nurture*: to care for and encourage the growth or development of.

Would the purpose of time-based emails not be to nurture a sales lead as well? Did anything about the example drip sequence above *not* seem to be nurturing the lead? It's no wonder there's so much confusion.

I think a more accurate distinction would be to call them *drip campaigns* and *reaction campaigns*. So let's stick with that. Reaction campaigns (nurture campaigns, to the conformists) are emails that are triggered by someone's behavior. It's significantly more complicated to set up than a drip campaign because your automation platform must *react* (see how that works?) to actions taken by the lead.

But while it may be more complicated, it is also more impactful, because you're delivering content explicitly designed to support the unique journey of the individual, and you're sending it when they are ready for it.

A reaction campaign could shake out like this:

- Day Zero—A first-time visitor to your website signs up for a free guide. An email is sent with a link to the guide. They are now a lead.
- Day Four—The lead visits the website a second time. Your system recognizes them (thanks to cookies) and sends them an email about an upcoming webinar.
- Day Thirty-one—The lead missed the webinar but finally watches the recording. An email is sent "from the salesperson" offering to give the lead a personal demo and a free trial.

You can see that if this were a drip campaign, the personal demo would have been sent, say, day seven. Unfortunately, that's before the prospect watched the webinar, a critical prerequisite to the demo. So he or she wasn't ready or willing to accept an invitation to a product demo, and the email goes unanswered.

This is not to suggest that drip campaigns are bad. Both campaign types can be extremely useful, depending on the situation. When used in concert, they will keep prospects engaged with your brand and help you close sales faster.

Email Types

There are fundamentally three types of emails you can send: the flyer, the newsletter, and the correspondence.

The Flyer

The flyer, as the name implies, is a straight-up advertisement email. Sometimes subscription-based (people sign up explicitly to receive coupons, discounts, and special offers), flyers are always image heavy and aggressively promote a product, service, or experience with strong calls to action.

The Newsletter

The newsletter, also known as an e-zine, is a recurring, subscription-based email that you send to people who have opted to receive it. They are typically image-heavy and will usually contain multiple stories or articles. Some may even have an advertisement or two sprinkled throughout. Often part of a long-term lead nurturing campaign, the primary goal of newsletters is to create top-of-mind awareness (TOMA) with both existing and prospective customers. It does this by delivering relevant educational or entertaining content.

The thing about building top-of-mind awareness is that you have to be continuously in someone's face to achieve it. And *that* notion makes many business owners shudder—at least, when it comes to email marketing. Look, I get it. The thought of bombarding your subscribers with high volumes of email conjures up images of angry, pitchfork-wielding clients and mass unsubscribes. But that's head trash—a belief stubbornly held onto, regardless of the facts.

The biggest myth in email marketing is the frequency with which you can (and should) email your list of subscribers. A few think it's once per week. Most think it's once per month. I've encountered some who think it's (gasp) once per quarter. This also happens to be one of the most common questions I am asked at any webinar, seminar, or workshop in which I've participated. "Mark, how often should I email my list?"

This question often derails the program because my answer, "As often as you possibly can," is often met with opposition.

But believe me when I say that if you can email your list weekly, you should do it weekly. If you can do it daily, do it daily. And if you can do it hourly—wait for it—do it hourly. Email frequency is big-time head trash, especially because few people who argue against me have ever tried it. They "just know" they would anger their list and get hundreds of unsubscribes.

The problem is that those people are looking at email frequency in isolation, when, in fact, one must consider frequency and relevancy in tandem. Frequency and relevancy—you can't consider one without the other.

If what you're emailing me is relevant content I enjoy, then I will welcome it, regardless of how frequently you send it. Yes, even if it's more than once per day. Don't believe me? I invite you to go to your inbox right now and see how often Facebook emails you.

Here's a screenshot of my inbox.

More ▾ 1–50 of many

Sender	Label	Date
Facebook	Inbox	Jul 25
Facebook	Inbox	Jul 25
Facebook	Inbox	Jul 25
Facebook	Inbox	Jul 24
Facebook	Inbox	Jul 24
Facebook	Inbox	Jul 23
Facebook	Inbox	Jul 23
Facebook	Inbox	Jul 23
Facebook	Inbox	Jul 23

As you can see, I'm getting an average of three emails per day from Facebook. And, I might add, that is after having already unsubscribed from many of the communication options to which Facebook defaults.

I know what you're thinking. *Well, I'm not Facebook.* Granted. But that doesn't matter. If Exxon emailed you daily with company updates, would you welcome the emails? Maybe you would if you were a shareholder; otherwise, probably not. The point is, it's not the size of your company—be it a Fortune 500 behemoth or a mom and pop shop from across the street—that determines the frequency with which you can email your list. It is 100 percent based on the quality of your content and the level of interest your subscribers have reading it.

Remember: newsletters are things people have opted to receive because they value their content. Within this framework, the only reason you should slow down your email frequency is if you aren't able to produce enough relevant, high-quality content to keep up the pace.

This part I cannot stress enough. It must be quality content. No one likes garbage. In fact, the only thing people dislike more than garbage is a lot of garbage. So, upping the frequency of garbage isn't going to do you any good.

I do have one caveat before you go back to the office and start shooting off an email every hour. You must replace the opt-out link (aka unsubscribe) with an opt-*down* link. The opt-down is a critical component of a high-frequency newsletter program, because inevitably you will have some people on your list who love your content but can't handle the load. That opt-down link will take subscribers to a page with email frequency options such as

- daily;
- weekly digest;
- monthly digest; or
- never again (unsubscribe).

I put this to the test in 2013 when I joined Remodelers Advantage, an international business consulting agency that works exclusively with remodelers. When I came onboard, they had a little over 22,000 email subscribers to the PowerTips Newsletter, which was sent out twice per month. Within six months, I increased our content production to twice *per week*—a significant increase in emails.

In two years, our list dropped to about 17,500, a net loss of 4,500 subscribers, or 20 percent. That may sound like a bad thing, but hold your horses. I'm happy to report that our sales conversions on our subscriber list *increased* by 230 percent. And *that* is the number that matters. You want your list converting into sales—period.

Consider this. If all it takes is a few more emails per month to make them quit me, then they don't value the content I'm delivering—which means they don't value the service I can offer them (since the content was *how to improve your business,* and we are consultants who help you improve your business).

And, obviously, if they don't value my services, then they never would have become paying customers. I can say that with absolute confidence, thanks to the opt-down link. To unsubscribe, they saw the choices and chose to not even receive a monthly digest.

In case you were wondering, I had about 2,500 people (14 percent) move themselves to the weekly or monthly digest options. This subset proved that they value my content, they just didn't want it twice a week.

So, as you can see, I'm okay with unsubscribes. I'd prefer to have a short list of future customers than a long list of timewasters and tire-kickers.

The Correspondence

The correspondence is meant to look like a one-on-one conversation. Similar to the Lucy Letter I described in Chapter Sixteen, it's a wonderful format that gives a personal feel to your mass email program. It encourages engagement with your readers and, as such, is my go-to when I'm looking to promote something. It should be noted that this format can also be used for your recurring subscriber emails. This works particularly well if you're the face of the brand and people are subscribing to hear from *you*. For example, "Hi John, A lot of my clients have been asking me about the new estate tax rules that have been put in place. So I thought I'd clear the air once and for all in this week's edition of Victoria's Take. Click here to read the post."

Mix and Match for Maximum Impact

One technique I've used with excellent results is combining formats. Here's how it works: Imagine you're a consultant putting on a seminar. The first email to your list is a flyer, expressly promoting the upcoming two-hour seminar, complete with program details, photos, and more. The second email is a correspondence *above* the original flyer email, in which you say something like, "Hi John, Yesterday I sent you information about my upcoming workshop (copied below). I wanted to follow-up personally because…"

As you can imagine, this one-two punch can make a big impression on the reader.

Email Anatomy–The Envelope

Regardless of format, frequency, or strategy, there's one thing all emails must do: get read. What's that saying? If an email falls in the forest, and no one is around to read it—I don't know. Something like that.

My point is, you could have the second coming of *War and Peace* inside, but if it doesn't get opened, no one will ever read it.

And that's why you must pay strict attention to the envelope. Just as with a physical letter, the email envelope is everything you see in your inbox before opening the email.

The envelope consists of three things:

1. The From Line
2. The Subject Line
3. The Snippet (aka the Pre-header)

Component One: The From Line

The from line is comprised of both the name *and* email address (two mutually exclusive elements). It will look something like this: John Doe <john@fluffydecks.com>.

This example, however, is not ideal when it comes to mass email marketing campaigns, since your list is comprised of both clients *and* strangers who have subscribed. Let's look at the name part first. It should either reinforce your brand or reinforce the subscription.

For example, instead of just John Doe, you would use either:

- John Doe with Fluffy Decks (reinforces your brand); or,
- Comfortable Living Weekly (reinforces the subscription).

On a side note (and as I mentioned earlier), you should seriously consider giving your newsletter and/or blog a compelling publication name. Don't just call it *Our Blog*. This not only improves open rates; it also improves subscription rates. Think about it. Wouldn't you be more likely to subscribe to something called *Comfortable Living Weekly* than *Our Blog*?

Okay, so that is the rule for the name part of the from line. Equally as important is the email address from which the email is delivered.

When it comes to subscription emails, something like newsletters@fluffydecks.com is a common choice. And while it's not the worst thing in the world, it is extremely impersonal. Your goal should be to build relationships with your list. I strongly recommend it come from *your* email address. That means that a better option for this company would be that they come from john@fluffydecks.com.

And this works regardless of whether the name reinforces the brand or the subscription. In fact, for the latter, you get the best of both worlds. You've reinforced the subscription, and they'll see your name in the email address.

The biggest pushback I get with regard to the email address is that people could reply to you. "My inbox is already overwhelmed. I can't have all that garbage hitting my inbox," is a common retort.

As far as I'm concerned, that's the cost of doing business. You can set up inbox rules and folders to manage the newsletter emails. Or create a second email account for you to manage. Whatever option you choose, the benefit of making yourself available far outweighs the inconvenience of an overfilled inbox.

Okay, so that's the first component of the envelope. Next.

Component Two: The Subject Line

This is the meat and potatoes of the whole show! It's the subject line that ultimately compels someone to stop in their tracks and open your email. It needs to be captivating! It's been said that when writing copy, you should spend 80 percent of your time on the headline (something I agree with very much). And the subject line of an email is the headline for what's inside.

Take a look at these two subject lines:

Option A:

John Doe with Fluffy Decks <john@fluffydecks.com>

This Week's Blog

Option B:

John Doe with Fluffy Decks <john@fluffydecks.com>

How Two Screws and Some Glue Saved My Marriage

Which would compel you to stop in your tracks and open the email?

Component Three: The Snippet (aka Pre-header)

The snippet is the preview text just below the subject line. Its purpose is to give the recipient a taste for what's inside so she can determine if he or she wants to open the email or not.

By default, the recipient's email client (Gmail, Outlook, Yahoo, etc.) grabs the first sentence or two of the body of your email and displays it, but some email marketing platforms have a custom text field that allows you to specify what your snippet text should be.

In the context of the email envelope, you should think of it as the subhead to your headline. Its goal is to expand on the subject line and entice the reader into wanting to read more.

So, using all the examples above, your email envelope would look something like this:

> John Doe with Fluffy Decks <john@fluffydecks.com>
> **How Two Screws and Some Glue Saved My Marriage**
> A DIY solution to the top item on everyone's honey-do list

What do you think? Does it sound like something worth opening? And as you can see, it took some work. As it should. The envelope is the most important part of your email, for, without a strong envelope, everything inside goes unseen. So invest time and energy in it.

In short, email marketing is the most effective way to build relationships with your target customers at scale. Unlike social media, where all the messaging is out there for the world to see, the inbox is private. Being invited into personal space is a very special thing. Don't squander the opportunity. It's your responsibility to respect the space and maintain that trust. Do so, and you will be well on your way to building a community of raving fans of your business.

TWENTY-THREE
MISSED OPPORTUNITIES

EVERY SINGLE TOUCH WITH ANOTHER HUMAN BEING IS an opportunity for your company to shine. More importantly, it's a chance to differentiate yourself from the competition. But there are a handful of situations where you can reap massive rewards, and you're ignoring them. Here are the top three opportunities that you are missing out on right now, and how to fix them.

Missed Opportunity One: Vacationing

Going on vacation? Great! The out-of-office reply is the single most overlooked opportunity a brand has to be remarkable. Firstly, it should go without mention that anytime you're going to be away from the office for a day or more, you should set up an automated email reply. I know it may seem silly to say, but I've honestly met more than a few people that have told me they never use an email autoresponder. This is a big no-no. You don't want people who email you to think you're ignoring them.

Okay, with that out of the way, let's discuss how you can turn this simple message into a marketing opportunity.

Does this look familiar?

I will be out of the office until August 27 with limited access to email. If this is urgent, please contact John Doe at John@fluffydecks.com or call (555) 555-5555.

How did you feel reading that? Not too warm and fuzzy, I would assume. Do you think John cares about his customers? Heck, John didn't even start the message with a hello.

Besides the fact that his tone is abrupt and rude, I think he's a liar. Unless John is climbing Mt. Everest, he most certainly has his phone and a signal. And phone + signal = email access. So I'm calling BS on the "I'll have limited access to email" comment.

These messages scream, "I'm off and don't want to be bothered. Leave me alone." And it mystifies me. All the work we put into building our brands, reputations, and relationships, and in the flash of an instant, we pronounce ourselves rude and thoughtless liars who can't be bothered.

You can do better than this—much better.

Start with the subject line. I just did a search on my inbox and found 1,046 emails with the phrase "out of office" in the subject line. Not really standing out from the crowd, are we?

Be different. This is a fundamental branding concept. Remember: every touch is an opportunity to show off your brand.

Try writing like a human. Imagine you're sitting on the beach, and you had to manually reply to the email when it came in. I doubt you would write "Out of Office Reply" in the subject line.

What if the subject line said, "Thanks for the email!" That sounds more human, don't you think? Or what about, "Sorry, I forget to tell you." That's more personal, wouldn't you agree?

Okay, great! You're already making a good impression, and the emailer hasn't even opened your reply yet.

Now, let's move on to the body of the email. Every out-of-office response must address two important things: when you'll be back, and how the person who wrote to you can get help if they need it.

1. When you'll be back

This seems easy enough, but pump the brakes for a moment. If you're going to be away for an extended period of time, like five days or more, then you probably shouldn't put the actual date you're returning. Odds are, your first day back will be nuts! You'll be playing catch-up all day long. How do you expect to get back to everyone who is waiting for a reply? Add a day or two to your return date and give yourself a fighting chance. If you're able to get back to someone sooner, great! This is a perfect time to under-promise and over-deliver.

2. How to get help

It's important to give the emailer another contact to reach out to, in case they need immediate assistance. But consider the circumstances in which someone may need immediate assistance. Some situations will be somewhat important. But one or two of them could be *four-alarm fire* important.

Be a caring and concerned representative of your brand, and show them you will always be there for them (well, within reason). Depending on your brand personality, perhaps something like this will work:

> Sorry, I must have forgotten to mention that I will be away on vacation until Tuesday, August 27.
>
> I promised my family that I would not be working (not even a little bit) during our time together, so I won't see your message until then.
>
> That being said, my kids know that sometimes disaster strikes. So if it's *really* important, please resend your email with *stop family time* in the subject line. This phrase will trigger an alert on my phone, and I will get back to you as soon as I possibly can.

A message like this is sure to make the emailer know how much you value them, and still make them think twice about bothering you with something trivial.

Finally, you should give them a gift. Hey, you're off on some tropical island sipping margaritas, and these poor people are knee deep in the daily grind. The least you could do is lessen the sting. Right?

Seriously, though, every communication is a marketing opportunity. Have a call to action. Give them a free download, access to resources, or just brighten their day with a funny video (preferably something that promotes or otherwise aligns with your brand). Use your imagination, and have fun with this.

Using these three components, let's see what our out-of-office email looks like now.

> **Subject:** I Guess I Goofed
> **Body:**
>
> I must have forgotten to mention that I will be away on vacation until Tuesday, August 27.
>
> Sorry about that.
>
> The thing is, I promised my family that I would not be working (not even a little bit) during our time together, so I won't see your message until then.
>
> That being said, my kids know that sometimes disaster strikes (they're understanding like that).
>
> So if it's *really* important, please resend your message with *stop family time* in the subject line. This phrase will trigger an alert on my phone, and I will get back to you as soon as I possibly can.
>
> If it's not *that* urgent, but it can't wait until I return, you can contact our office manager, Jerry Smith, at 555-465-1125.

> If neither of those are the case, then I guess it can wait until I get back on the twenty-seventh!
>
> By the way, we're an exhibitor at the Home and Garden Show being held at the convention center on September 12–14. Think you'd like to come? If so, click here to print a free pass to the event, with our compliments. I hope to see you there!
>
> Talk to you soon,
> John Doe
> Fluffy Decks, LLC

So what do you think? How are you feeling? Do you think John is genuinely concerned about you? Do you feel like you will be taken care of?

I use this tactic all the time, and the responses are phenomenal. Besides leaving a great impression with clients and prospects, I receive loads of compliments on having such an honest message.

What's more, I've had my out-of-office emails forwarded hundreds of times. (How's that for free advertising?)

And if you're wondering if anyone has ever used my emergency rule, the answer is yes. Twice. One didn't count because that person just wanted to tell me, *immediately*, how impressed he was with my out-of-office email. He wrote, "Sorry, Mark. Please don't stop family time on my account. I just had to tell you how blown away I am by your autoresponder. Thanks for all you do. Now, go enjoy that family of yours! I'll talk to you when you're back."

The other time was a legitimate business emergency. It was a long time ago, when I co-owned a remodeling company. We were adding a skylight, and my guys cut it into the roof four feet to the left of where it was supposed to be. As you can imagine, when the homeowner came home, she wasn't happy with the hole in her ceiling. She tried calling my cell phone, but I had the *do not disturb* on, so she was sent straight to voicemail. (Can you imagine what she must have been feeling that very moment when the phone went straight to voicemail?)

Her next move was to send me an email, and she most likely saw my out-of-office reply seconds after hitting the send button.

This means that by the time I saw the *stop family time* email come through, it would have been her third attempt to reach me— a third attempt *after* having come home to an erroneous hole in her ceiling.

And, guess what? She started the email with an apology. Here's a woman who was upset. And by upset, I mean mouth-foaming angry. And she was apologizing to me because she felt bad for interrupting family time.

It turned out to be a great tool to defuse the situation. Naturally, after getting her email, I dropped everything and called. She answered the phone expressing gratitude, and apologized again for the interruption.

I don't even want to think about how this situation would have gone down if, after having been sent straight to my voicemail, she would have received the standard out-of-office reply from me.

Missed Opportunity Two: The Thank-You Page

You've done your job. The copy is compelling, and the offer (called a *lead magnet*) is irresistible. Couple that with your strong call to action, and the prospect has no choice. He *must* fill out the form and get your free download, *The Guide of Awesome Stuff*. You've got him right where you want him.

Unfortunately, the next thing he sees after submitting the form is a page that says, "Thanks! Your guide is on the way. Check your inbox."

Bummer. Another missed opportunity.

Thank-you pages are the pages on your website that you send people to after they submit a form or complete a purchase. It also happens to be the most underutilized page on a website and, subsequently, a massive opportunity missed.

In his book *Mastering Store Merchandising: A How-to Guide for Retailers*, merchandising expert Joe Baer writes, "Driving impulse purchases is a key business strategy to drive volume and store sales. Create an area adjacent to the checkout area [to] tempt customers with something they weren't expecting but suddenly need to have." Joe calls this area adjacent to the checkout the "impulse zone."

I'm sure you've fallen victim to this merchandising strategy more than once.

While it's technically *after* checkout, the thank-you page is the impulse zone of your marketing funnel. The prospect has already engaged with your brand, "paid" for valuable information (with personal information as the currency), and is primed and ready to give you more. You must continue probing while the iron is hot.

You could use it to build out the prospect profile further. For example, if they give you a name and email address for a whitepaper download, the thank-you page could say something like, "Your whitepaper is on the way! Would you also like a free copy of our eBook?" And here, they'll need to give more information like job title, company name, and phone number.

Alternately, you could probe for purchase intent. For example, after downloading *The Guide to Home Buying*, a real estate agent could have the thank-you page ask when they plan to purchase in exchange for a market outlook report.

The possibilities are limited only by your imagination.

Missed Opportunity Three: 404 Error Pages

You've inevitably stumbled across the dreaded 404 error at one time or another. It's the page every website displays when a visitor attempts to visit a URL that doesn't exist. It's an incredibly frustrating experience.

Consider that whatever link you find, it speaks to you. Excitement and anticipation build as you move your mouse over it. On the other end of this click is going to be the answer to all your problems. You click, and in nanoseconds, your hopes and dreams are destroyed by a horrifying "page not found" error.

And as frustrating as this is for the visitor, it's much worse for you, the website owner. You've not only disappointed a potential customer; you've also portrayed yourself as incompetent. *Guy can't even keep his website up and running without errors,* they'll think.

The bad news is you can't prevent 404s from happening. Links go bad over time. It's inevitable. The good news is that you can convert this bad experience into a good one. In fact, if you do it right, your 404 error page could even increase your conversions, boost revenue, and turn those lost visitors into loyal customers.

How? Let's break it down. At minimum, a 404 page should do two things: let the visitor know the page they are looking for is not here, and recommend a next step. A strong 404 page, however, will also tie into your brand, be memorable, and have a call to action. Your ultimate goal is to reengage your visitor so they stick around and explore your website.

Tie into Your Brand

I've only mentioned this 6,000 times already. And here's 6,001. Every interaction with your brand, no matter how small or insignificant, must support your positioning and convey your brand personality. Consistency is critical. And the 404 error page is no different.

Be Memorable

Remember the key to word of mouth? Break a schema. Do something wonderfully unexpected, and you will be rewarded. One website I visited had a playable Space Invaders game on their 404 page. The message read, "Oh no! Space Invaders destroyed this page! Take revenge on them!" The space invaders were organized to spell out the company name. And here's the most creative part: if you score over a thousand points, you win a discount code. Having someone earn a discount (as opposed to just handing it out) virtually guarantees they will spend money with you.

Another website had a music video featuring the company's owner as the lead singer and his kids playing the instruments. The song was one he wrote himself, apologizing for the missing web page. A memorable experience, indeed.

Have a Call to Action

You should always have a CTA. Without one, the page is nothing more than a dead end. And a dead end means you can say bye-bye to the visitor, who's off to Google to find the answer elsewhere. Even if it's something as simple as a search field or a link to a help page, it's better than nothing.

But I would recommend getting creative. Take a look at the Internet Movie Database. IMDB.com is the largest source of information on movies, TV, and celebrities. Their 404 page pulls quotes from movies and modifies them to suit the context of the missing page. It's very funny, and the call to action is a link to the quoted movie, keeping you engaged and (most importantly) on the website.

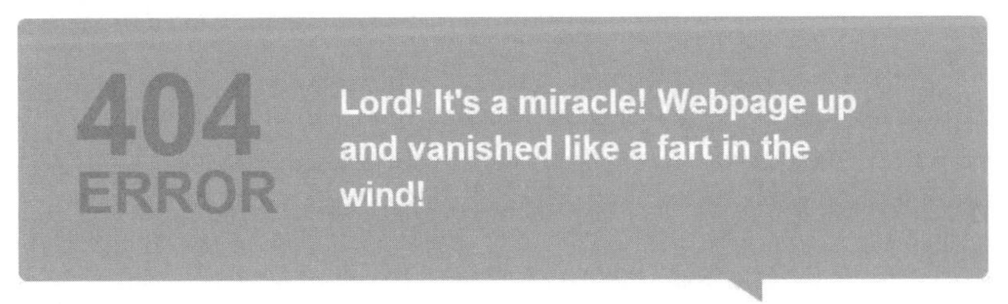

Or consider turning this experience into a list-building opportunity. Imagine apologizing for the missing page and making amends with a free gift—something like, "Sorry you didn't find what you were looking for. Let me send you this *Awesome Guide of Stuff* to make up for it."

To sum up, the 404 error page is a chance to shine. For existing fans, it will remind them why they love you, and it will show first-time visitors why they should. Don't squander the opportunity. For inspiration, I've included a list of great 404 pages on BeTheLobster.com/inspire404.

TWENTY-FOUR
SPLIT TESTING

WHEN I WAS A KID, I WOULD TAKE MY TOYS APART TO SEE how they worked. It drove my parents bonkers. I remember one remote control car in particular that didn't make it two days. My dad had some choice words to say about that one. I think that's one of the reasons I love marketing so much. It's like looking into people's brains to see how they work.

Now, you may not be as curious about human psychology as I am, but I'm sure you are serious about getting superior results from your marketing. And the only way to do that is to get serious about split testing.

Also known as A/B testing, a split test is exactly what it sounds like: you make two versions of a component, such as an email subject line, and see which version performs better.

The metric that defines success is usually obvious and determined by the component you are testing. In the case of a subject line, it would be email open rates. In the case of a call to action button, it would be clicks. And so on. But sometimes you do need to explicitly define what metric you're looking to improve upon. For example, social media posts can be judged based on clicks, shares, likes, etc.

The mechanics of executing a split test is dependent in large part on the platforms and technologies you use, and as such is far beyond the scope of what I can discuss here. But even more important than executing the test is interpreting the results.

Now, you may be thinking, *This is just comparing two results. What's so hard about that?* Unfortunately, there's a very common misstep that is made when evaluating the results of a split test. And it goes something like this: "I ran an A/B split test on my last email, changing the subject line in hopes of increasing my open rates. The results were pretty good. Email A had an open rate of 32.7 percent, and email B had an open rate of 29.1 percent. That's a 3.6 percent improvement."

Sounds right, right? But what if I told you that the improvement was actually 12.4 percent? Let me explain. What is being reported in the example is the *absolute* difference between the two open rates. Absolute difference is defined as the real number difference between the two results. In other words, it's just subtraction: A minus B.

So what's wrong with that? Nothing in and of itself. But the absolute difference only shows you how each performed in the overall campaign.

To understand the significance of the improvement, you need to compare them to each other.

You do this by looking at the *relative* difference between the test results. Also known as *percentage change*, the relative difference between two numbers lets you see the scale impact of your test.

The percentage change formula is (A – B) / B

So if we plug in the example numbers above, we get

(32.7 – 29.1) / 29.1 = 0.124, or 12.4 percent.

What's the Point?

It may sound like fuzzy math to some. To others it may sound like an attempt to inflate the results. I can appreciate that. The truth is that both numbers are valuable, and you should calculate both when looking at the results of your split test, because they will give you two distinct but useful statements:

Absolute change statement: We received 3.6 percent more opens with subject line A.

Relative change statement: For every email opened using subject line B, there are 12.4 percent more opens happening with subject line A.

Remember your goal in all of this: to continually improve your marketing so that you may get the best possible return on your efforts. Use the results, and common sense, to make the right decisions, and you will see a noticeable change in your success.

TWENTY-FIVE
MARKETING THROUGH CRISIS

THIS BOOK WAS NEARLY COMPLETE. IN FACT, I WAS preparing to send it to an editor to make sure I didn't misuse a semicolon when I heard the report that COVID-19 had entered the United States.

Within weeks, the world as we knew it had changed. The entire country was virtually closed for business, and business owners everywhere were scrambling to survive. Needless to say, I shelved the book and began working with my team to help the industry get through the crisis.

The thing about a crisis—any crisis—is that what you do in the short-term is critical to your ability to survive now and thrive later. For some, the best choice is to go to the Winchester, have a pint, and wait for all of this to blow over. For everyone else (who's not waiting out a zombie apocalypse), I'll share the short-term steps (as they relate to marketing) that you should take at the onset of a crisis.

But first, I need to emphasize that being optimistic is as important as taking action. A crisis is always an opportunity.

Don't mistake this sentiment as my saying that you should be *opportunistic*. I'm not talking about exploiting a crisis for gain.

But crisis *is* an opportunity reset your business. Inevitably, those who come out the other side will have healthier processes, cleaner systems, and perhaps even new services to offer as a result of the actions taken to weather the storm.

I have seen many companies get leaner and stronger after crises, including the dot-com bubble burst in 2000, the great recession of

2007, and, most recently, the COVID-19 pandemic in 2020. Case in point, this book didn't have a chapter on crisis marketing before the pandemic hit.

As author Robert Brault defined it: An optimist is someone who figures that taking a step backward after taking a step forward is not a disaster, it's a cha-cha. So when crisis strikes, put on your Latin dance shoes, stay optimistic, and look at it as an opportunity for improvement.

Be an Icon

In the days that followed the shutdown, many of our members reached out to me, asking what they should do with their marketing. Should they stop? Should they invest more? What should the message be? And so on.

I came up with these four steps to help them: Inventory, Communicate, Offer Yourself, and Next Phase (ICON).

Inventory

When your company faces a crisis, you must immediately audit all messaging. You need to take an inventory of what you have out there and ensure that it is not suddenly insensitive, seemingly opportunistic, or flat-out bad advice. For example, *It's finger lickin' good* isn't the best advice when there's a pandemic. People don't need to be encouraged to touch their faces, much less lick their fingers.

Be sure to check your existing social media posts. Things change fast in crisis. Be prepared to take down anything that may have once been acceptable. One remodeler I know made a funny video of a bored family wearing masks lying around a cramped living room. It looked like Salvador Dali's *Persistence of Memory* (the painting with the melted clocks). It was very funny. Even the dog was wearing a mask.

But suddenly, there was a mask shortage, and the government was asking people to donate masks to help. His video turned into an offensive waste of a much-needed resource overnight. Fortunately, he took it down before any damage was done.

Also, be sure to check all yet-to-be-delivered messaging. Automation is a wonderful "set it and forget it" tool until crisis hits. Revisit your drip campaigns, auto-responders, and prescheduled media. I was one of thousands who received the unfortunate "Never a Better Time to Fly" drip email from Spirit Airlines on March 12. Not a great message to be sending, wouldn't you agree?

Spirit apologized, citing that this email had been written months earlier. Don't let this happen to you.

Communicate

You need to convey what it is you are doing to cope with the situation at hand with everyone, existing clients, employees, vendors, trade partners, and other key stakeholders first. They have a vested interest in your operations and need to know that you are in control. Then communicate the necessary information to the community at large—aka your future clients.

Offer Yourself

Public relations should be your top priority when crisis hits. Defined as the state of the relationship between the public and a company, public relations is ultimately about empathy. It's about genuinely caring about the well-being of the community.

A great example of how a company can offer itself during a crisis comes from the 1983 comedy *Mr. Mom,* starring Michael Keaton and Teri Garr, who play a couple hit hard by a tanking economy. Jack Butler (Keaton) is laid off due to cutbacks. His wife, Caroline, a stay-at-home mom and former ad exec, is thrust back into the workforce when she's able to land a job before Jack (making him the stay-at-home "mom").

There is a scene in which Caroline pitches an ad for the president of Schooner Tuna, the agency's largest account. Caroline has just summarized how Schooner Tuna's last two campaigns, one giving away free glassware and the other giving away free trips to Hawaii, failed miserably.

Naturally, the president is none too happy with the history lesson, grunting, "I hope to hell you're making a point." Caroline states that she is in fact making a point – times are tough and housewives need his help, not his gimmicks. She asserts that if you "show them that you really care about their problems…you'll win their loyalty." She ultimately recommends that the advertisement should be him, the company president, making a heartfelt statement that he's reducing the price of their tuna until the crisis is over.

Needless to say, Mr. Humphrey loves the idea, and Caroline wins the project.

The point here isn't to go out and slash prices. The takeaway is that if you show you care, you'll win their loyalty.

How you show it depends on your role. What role does your brand play in your target's lives? First explore all the ways you fit into their lives, then find ways you can help or be useful.

During the COVID-19 crisis, some distillers converted their equipment and began turning whiskey and gin into hand sanitizer. In contrast, Disney Parks released fan-favorite secret recipes like their Mickey Mouse-shaped beignets and *Toy Story* Land's grilled cheese sandwich so that families could enjoy magic moments at home.

Always start with your target. Consider the challenges they are facing and how your company can help. Like Caroline said, show them you really care about their problems and you'll win their loyalty.

Next Phase

An inevitable byproduct of a crisis is an economic recession. Once you've completed the first three steps of ICON, you must start planning for the next phase. You have a marketing plan, but odds are that plan is out the window. It's time to go back to the drawing board and craft a new plan for the remainder of the year.

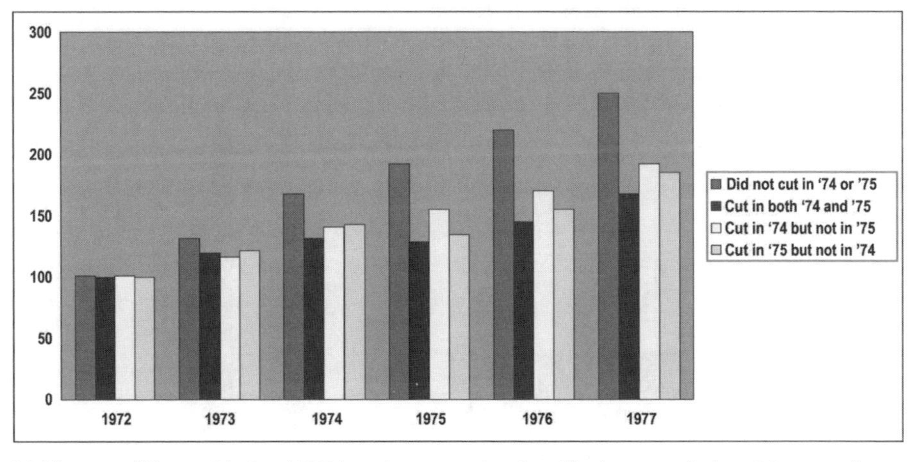

Meldrum and Fewsmith, Inc (1979) study to examine the effectiveness of advertising on sales during the 1974-1975 recession.

Obey the first commandment of marketing: Thou shalt not stop marketing during slow times. Many studies have been conducted on the impact of marketing during a recession, and all the results point to one undeniable fact. Companies that continue marketing through it come out many times stronger than those that do not. The three graphs from the recessions of the '70s, '80s, and '90s show just that.

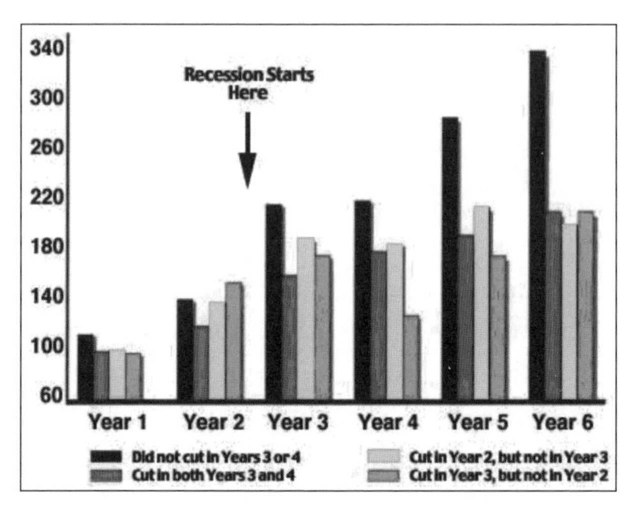

McGraw-Hill Research's Laboratory of Advertising Performance study on the effect of advertising and sales during the 1981-82 recession.

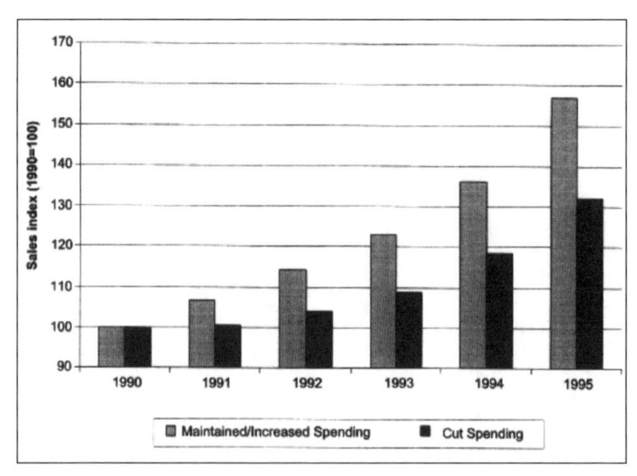

Thomas Kamber (2002) study on the effect of advertising on sales over a 6-year period that encompassed the 1990-91 recession

That being said, do not mistake this commandment to mean thou shalt not *cut your marketing budget* during slow times. While it's true that some companies *increase* spending during a recession (and reap the benefits after), it's not necessarily required to succeed these days. And while you should make every effort to, at minimum, maintain your current budget, it is still possible to cut and continue an effective marketing effort.

Technology has given modern marketers a significant advantage when it comes to reaching audiences on small budgets. So if you find that you *must* cut your budget, I recommend cutting three things.

1. Cut what isn't possible or realistic (like a networking event during a pandemic).
2. Cut what hasn't been performing.
3. Cut what is difficult to measure the success of.

This may seem obvious at first glance, but you'd be surprised. A knee-jerk reaction for many is to start cutting by expenditure, ceasing expensive campaigns regardless of how well they perform. Don't give in to the temptation. Marketing isn't an expense. It's an investment. And with all investments, you should expect multiples on the dollar in return. Cutting something that gives you a good ROI is just bad business.

Increase, maintain, or cut. You'll have to make the decision that is right for you. But whatever decision you make, do not stop marketing.

TWENTY-SIX
GOING IT ALONE

The world needs ditch diggers, too.

—Judge Smails, Caddyshack

I USED TO RUN A MARKETING ROUNDTABLES PROGRAM. Sometimes called a *mastermind group*, a roundtable is a group of like-minded professionals who get together to share experiences and help one another improve. It's like having your own advisory board. It's a powerful thing, indeed.

At the time, I facilitated two groups of ten. We met virtually every month and in person twice per year. Two of the twenty members were business owners who also wore the marketing hat. Three were marketers-slash-office managers. The rest were full-time marketing professionals. But all of them had one thing in common: they were the only person in the company responsible for marketing.

Most of the challenges shared in our time together were rooted in a lack of support. It's understandable. Many small businesses simply don't have the budget to staff a marketing team, so they operate with a marketing department of one.

It's a lonely place to be.

In our roundtables meetings, many of the stories shared contained words like *challenging*, *overwhelmed*, *stressful*, and *impossible*. But behind those words of frustration lay the answer: stop trying to do it all yourself.

Marketing is more complex today than any other time in history. The list of disciplines and specializations are enough to make one's head spin: social media, copywriting, graphic design, website development, SEO, pay-per-click, email marketing, analytics, research, affiliate marketing, branding, content, events, video, media planning, public relations—and that's just off the top of my head.

Business owners expect so much from one marketing employee. But one person cannot handle everything. The way to shine as a solo marketer is to accept the fact that you can't do it all, let go, and outsource many of the tasks that come your way. Easier said than done.

Believe me, I know. I'm the greatest offender of all. So much so that, over the past twenty years, I've taught myself to do everything from web development to video editing to graphic design. And while I'm happy that I now have a repertoire of proficiencies on which to lean, I wonder how much farther I could have gone had I spent my time on strategy and planning instead of watching YouTube videos on how to use Adobe Premiere.

So why did I resist outsourcing at every turn? I had three misguided reasons.

1. Keeping costs low
2. Desire to control the project every step of the way
3. Bad experiences with outsourced help

The first one was the most ridiculous. The truth is that it's oftentimes more cost-efficient to send a task to a specialist who lives and breathes the discipline. Maybe it's not on a tit-for-tat cost of delivery basis, but when you factor in time (because you'll be able to work on other things while it's getting done) and expertise, odds are you're coming out ahead.

Still, the fear of hiring a dud coupled with the need to keep control are difficult feelings to overcome. To help you decide what to outsource, ask yourself three questions.

1. Can the results be drastically improved if I hire an expert?
Consider your skillset against what a professional will deliver and estimate the amount of lift you can expect in the outcome. Be sure to take into account what's at stake when determining the value.

2. Are there more important things I can be doing to move the company forward?
Your time is the more valuable than money. If there is anything on your plate that only you can do (or you can do most effectively) and will have a bigger impact on the company's success, you should be focusing on that instead.

3. Is it even necessary?
It's easy to catch shiny object syndrome, especially after reading a great book on marketing (wink). But don't fall victim. As Jim Collins points out in his book, *Good to Great*, stop-doing lists are as important as to-do lists. If it's a task you're considering outsourcing, stop and ask yourself if you even need to be doing it at all.

Answer these three questions honestly and deliberately, and you will be able to effectively identify the tasks and projects you should keep in-house and those you should outsource.

Unfortunately, all the outsourcing in the world can't fix your greatest challenge. You're still a marketing department of one. Without having others to share your challenges, to bounce ideas off of, or flat-out ask for help, you will never reach your full potential. So with that in mind, I created the *Be the Lobster* community. It's a place where small business marketers can come together and help one another navigate the unique challenges that solo marketers face. I hope you'll join the community because, if there's one thing I learned in my years as a facilitator, it's that isolation is the enemy of success. To join the conversation, visit BeTheLobster.com/facebook.

Conclusion

Oh, just one more thing.

—Lieutenant Columbo, ***Columbo***

MY FAVORITE TV DETECTIVE IS, HANDS DOWN, COLUMBO, played by the late, great Peter Falk. I've seen every one of the sixty-seven episodes many times over (as well as the two made-for-TV movies that preceded the series). His trademark false exit is stuff of legend. This is where the seemingly absentminded sleuth walks away from an informal interrogation, only to stop short when he "suddenly remembers" to ask one more question. It's a highly effective tactic, because the killer has let his guard down, thinking he's successfully parried the probing detective's attack. The relaxed posture opens the killer up to making a mistake.

Similarly, you may be feeling a sense of relief now that the book is over. You've completed your positioning statement, gotten your messaging squared away, and created a strategic marketing plan.

Don't be the killer in *Columbo*!

This is no time to relax. The book may be over, but your work is just beginning.

Don't get me wrong. I know how much work you have put in to get here. You earned a break. In fact, if any of my movie references went over your head, now would be a good time to get caught up. Like I said in the introduction, I never quote bad flicks. Pop some popcorn, kick back, and enjoy.

But tomorrow, we get back to work. Be sure to visit BeTheLobster.com. There you will find additional tools and resources beyond what I've referenced in this book, from an ROI calculator to a competitor analysis workbook, to recommended reading, to where you can get free images for your blog posts. You will also find the hidden chapter of this book: Chapter 9-3/4—"Mystery Marketing to Engage Your Customer."

And you can access it all for three easy payments of $49.95.

Just kidding. It's my gift to you. I hope that these resources, along with the *Be the Lobster* community, will help you keep your marketing department running at peak performance.

And so, in the immortal words of my man Deadpool, "Okay, guys. Let's get out there and make a difference. [whispering] You know what to do."

APPENDIX A

LIST OF INSPIRATION: PERSONALITY TRAITS

Accessible
Active
Adaptable
Admirable
Adventurous
Agreeable
Alert
Amiable
Anticipative
Appreciative
Approachable
Articulate
Aspiring
Athletic
Attractive
Balanced
Benevolent
Brilliant
Calm
Capable
Captivating
Cautious
Caring
Challenging
Charismatic
Charming
Cheerful
Clean
Clear-headed
Clever
Colorful
Companionly
Compassionate
Conciliatory
Confident
Conscientious
Considerate
Constant
Contemplative
Cooperative
Courageous
Courteous
Creative
Cultured
Curious
Daring
Debonair
Decent
Decisive
Dedicated
Deep
Dignified
Directed
Disciplined
Discreet
Dramatic
Dutiful
Dynamic
Earnest
Ebullient
Educated
Efficient
Elegant
Eloquent
Empathetic
Energetic
Enthusiastic
Esthetic
Exclusive
Exciting
Extraordinary
Fair
Faithful
Farsighted
Firm
Flexible
Focused
Forceful
Forgiving
Forthright
Freethinking
Friendly
Fun-loving
Gallant
Generous
Gentle
Genuine
Good-natured
Gracious
Hardworking
Healthy
Hearty
Helpful
Heroic
High-minded
Honest
Honorable
Humble
Humorous
Idealistic
Imaginative
Impressive
Incisive
Incorruptible
Independent
Individualistic
Innovative
Inoffensive
Insightful
Insouciant
Intelligent
Intuitive
Invulnerable
Kind
Knowledgeable
Leader
Leisurely
Liberal
Logical
Lovable
Loyal
Lyrical
Magnanimous
Many-sided

Masculine
Mature
Methodical
Meticulous
Moderate
Modest
Multi-leveled
Neat
Objective
Observant
Open
Optimistic
Orderly
Organized
Original
Painstaking
Passionate
Patient
Patriotic
Peaceful
Perceptive
Perfectionist
Personable
Persuasive
Playful
Polished
Popular
Practical
Precise
Principled
Profound
Protective
Providential
Prudent
Punctual
Purposeful
Rational
Realistic
Reflective
Relaxed
Reliable
Resourceful
Respectful
Responsible
Responsive
Reverential
Romantic
Rustic
Sage
Sane
Scholarly
Scrupulous
Secure
Selfless
Self-critical
Self-defacing
Self-denying
Self-reliant
Self-sufficient
Sensitive
Sentimental
Seraphic
Serious
Sexy
Sharing
Shrewd
Simple
Skillful
Sober
Sociable
Solid
Sophisticated
Spontaneous
Sporting
Stable
Steadfast
Steady
Stoic
Strong
Studious
Suave
Subtle
Sweet
Sympathetic
Systematic
Tasteful
Teacherly
Thorough
Tidy
Tolerant
Tractable
Trusting
Understanding
Undogmatic
Upright
Upscale
Urbane
Venturesome
Vivacious
Warm
Well-bred
Well-read
Well-rounded
Winning
Wise
Witty
Youthful

APPENDIX B

THE DEFINITIVE LIST OF MARKETING TACTICS

For an Excel-based spreadsheet that allows you to change scores and weight each of the five factors, visit BeTheLobster.com/tactics-spreadsheet.

GRADING SCALE	
Time to Launch **(L)**	1 = little to no time – 5 = major investment of time
Time to Outcome **(O)**	1 = immediate ROI – 5 = significant time before realizing returns
Potency **(P)**	1 = low impact – 5 = high impact. (Level of positive impact)
Cost **(C)**	1 = little to no cost – 5 = very expensive
Skill **(S)**	1 = easy – 5 = expert

TACTIC	L	O	P	C	S	SCORE
Affiliate Marketing	3	2	3	2	3	3.4
Billboard Advertising	3	3	1	4	5	1.8
Blog Commenting	2	5	1	1	2	2.4
Blogging	2	5	4	1	3	3.0
Branded Apps	4	4	3	4	4	2.2
Bulletin Boards and Directories (online)	1	1	1	1	1	3.6
Canvassing	1	2	1	2	2	3.2
Circulars	2	2	2	3	2	3.3
Classified Ads	1	1	1	1	4	3.0
Cold Calling	1	3	1	1	2	3.1
Contests and Sweepstakes	3	5	1	4	4	1.6
Digital Advertising	2	2	1	3	3	2.7
Direct Mail (Ads)	2	2	2	3	3	3.1
Direct Mail	2	3	3	1	3	3.5
Door Hangers / Flyers	1	1	1	1	2	3.5
E-books	3	2	3	2	3	3.4
Educational Workshops	5	2	5	3	3	2.8
Email (Broadcast)	2	1	3	2	3	3.7
Email (drip campaigns)	4	2	4	1	4	3.2
Email Signature	1	1	1	1	1	3.6
eNewsletters (subscribers)	2	4	3	1	3	3.2
Events (hosting - ie seminars/workshops)	4	2	4	5	3	2.5
Free Consultations	1	2	4	1	3	4.1

TACTIC	L	O	P	C	S	SCORE
Guest Posting	4	3	1	1	3	2.5
Joint Ventures	3	1	4	1	3	3.9
Landing Pages	2	1	4	2	4	3.6
Memberships (associations/clubs)	1	5	1	1	1	2.6
Native Advertisements	2	1	3	2	2	3.9
Networking	1	5	1	1	2	2.5
Open House	2	1	2	2	2	3.6
Pay Per Click	3	1	2	3	4	2.8
Personalized Letters and Email Messages	1	1	3	1	1	4.5
Podcasting	2	5	2.5	2	4	2.4
Press Releases	1	1	1	1	3	3.3
Print Ads	3	2	2	5	4	2.2
Promotional Products	1	4	1	2	1	2.9
Publish a Book	5	5	5	5	3	1.7
Published Articles	2	3	3	1	3	3.5
Radio Advertisements	3	3	2	4.5	5	1.9
Radius Mailing	2	2	2	3.5	4	2.8
Referrals / Word-of-Mouth	1	1	5	1	2	4.8
Sales Collateral	2	5	1	3	3	2.0
Search Engine Optimization (SEO)	5	5	4	3	4	1.9
Signage (Lawn Signs, etc.)	3	5	3	4	5	1.8
SME Interviews (subject-matter expert)	5	3	4	1	5	2.3
SMS (texting)	1	1	2	2.5	5	2.8
Social Media	1	5	2	1	4	2.5
Speaking (conferences/workshops)	3	1	3	2	4	3.2
Sponsorships	1	1	1	4	1	3.0
Telemarketing	1	2	1	3	3	2.8
Television Commercials	5	4	2	5	5	1.3
Testimonials / Case Studies	2	1	5	1	4	4.0
Trade Shows	5	4	2	5	3	1.6
Vehicle Wraps	2	4	2	4	3	2.5
Video Marketing (online)	3	5	3	3	4	2.2
Webinars	4	2.5	4	2	3	3.2
Website	5	5	4	4	4	1.7

Suggested Reading

These books offer sage advice for dominating your market. I wouldn't be where I am today without them. Most are marketing books, but some are just flat out good business books. I've also dropped in some of my guilty pleasure books for you,* because all work and no play makes for a burnt-out business owner. (All three were made into movies, but the books are better.)

Influence: The Psychology of Persuasion by Robert B. Cialdini, Ph.D.

Scientific Advertising by Claude Hopkins

Hey Whipple, Squeeze This: A Guide to Creating Great Advertising by Luke Sullivan

The New Rules of Marketing and PR: How to Use Social Media, Online Video, Mobile Applications, Blogs, News Releases, and Viral Marketing to Reach Buyers Directly by David Meerman Scott

Purple Cow: Transform Your Business by Being Remarkable by Seth Godin

The Tipping Point: How Little Things Can Make a Big Difference by Malcolm Gladwell

Never Split the Difference: Negotiating as if Your Life Depended on It by Chris Voss

I, Robot by Isaac Asimov*

Employee Engagement: Lessons from the Mouse House by Pete Blank

Good to Great: Why Some Companies Make the Leap and Others Don't by Jim Collins

The Guerrilla Marketing Handbook by Jay Levinson and Seth Godin

Built to Last: Successful Habits of Visionary Companies by Jim Collins

Public Speaking to Win: The Original Formula to Speaking with Power by Dale Carnegie

The Shining by Stephen King*

Ogilvy on Advertising by David Ogilvy

The Culture of Success by Steven J. Anderson

Built to Sell: Creating a Business That Can Thrive Without You by John Warrillow

The Automatic Customer: Creating a Subscription Business in Any Industry by John Warrillow

Get in the Game: How To Create Rapid Financial Results And Lasting Cultural Change by Rich Armstrong and Steve Baker

Ready Player One by Ernest Cline*

Positioning: The Battle for Your Mind by Al Ries and Jack Trout

Content Inc.: How Entrepreneurs Use Content to Build Massive Audiences and Create Radically Successful Businesses by Joe Pulizzi

Hooked: How to Build Habit-Forming Products by Nir Eyal

Death by Meeting: A Leadership Fable about Solving the Most Painful Problem in Business by Patrick Lencioni

The Great Game of Business by Jack Stack

Exactly What to Say: The Magic Words for Influence and Impact by Phil M. Jones

Suggested Watching

I warned you, didn't I? While I hope this book has exceeded your expectations and provided you with the tools you need to dominate your market, I also hope you enjoyed the subtle and not-so-subtle nods to a few of the films in my video library. If you're wondering if you caught them all, here they are (by order of appearance). And if you haven't seen them, *you should.*

Pulp Fiction (2004), directed by Quentin Tarantino, p. xi

The Big Lebowski (1998), directed by Joel Coen and Ethan Coen, p. xi

Citizen Kane (1941), directed by Orson Welles, p. xi

Captain Marvel (2019), directed by Anna Boden and Ryan Fleck, p. 1

The Princess Bride (1987), directed by Rob Reiner, pp. 1, 7, 61

Donnie Brasco (1997), directed by Mike Newell, pp. 2, 41

Glengarry Glen Ross (1992), directed by James Foley, pp. 3, 24

Back to the Future (1985), directed by Robert Zemeckis, p. 4

Wall Street (1987), directed by Oliver Stone, p. 6

Avengers: Infinity War (2018), directed by Anthony Russo and Joe Russo, pp. 20, 21, 27

A Few Good Men (1992), directed by Rob Reiner, p. 31

Pirates of the Caribbean: The Curse of the Black Pearl (2003), directed by Gore Verbinski, p. 53

The Godfather (1972), directed by Francis Ford Coppola, pp. 68, 167

I, Robot (2004), directed by Alex Proyas, p. 73

Cast Away (2000), directed by Robert Zemeckis, p. 75

Star Wars: Episode IV (1977), directed by George Lucas, p. 102

Field of Dreams (1989), directed by Phil Alden Robinson, p. 113

The Shawshank Redemption (1994), directed by Frank Darabont, p. 135

Shawn of the Dead (2004), directed by Edgar Wright, p. 141

Mr. Mom (1983), directed by Stan Dragoti, p. 144

Caddyshack (1980), directed by Harold Ramis, p. 149

Deadpool (2016), directed by Tim Miller, p. 154

About the Author

Mark Harari is a writer, speaker, trainer, and outspoken critic of the nominative determinism theory. (This is the hypothesis that a person's name influences what they do for a living.) Although it's true that a disproportionate number of dentists are named Dennis, he thinks it's coincidental, and the theory is silly.

Mark's marketing career ...hmm. Well, moving on.

Mark's marketing career began over twenty years ago with a freelance side hustle while selling lumber full-time, and he never looked back, having since helped hundreds of small businesses rock their marketing.

He is the recipient of numerous marketing awards in many categories, including video, web design, print advertising, and copywriting. They include three prestigious Muse Creative awards, an IAC award, three AVA Digital awards, and two MarCom International awards.

He firmly believes that learning should be fun, failure is critical to success, and when faced with the choice, you should leave the gun and take the cannoli.

In his free time, he enjoys watching hockey, going to the gym, fantasy football, playing soccer with his daughter, golfing with his son, collecting movie memorabilia, taking his wife to dinner, and watching movies with their dog, Max. (No, Deb, not in that order.)

If you want to chat, don't search him out on Google. He does not own a gym and doesn't look much like that guy unless you squint... a lot. You're better off connecting with him via LinkedIn at www.linkedin.com/in/markharari.